Editor **NICK PULFORD**

Cover designed by Jay Vincent

Designed by David Dew

David Baxter	Liam Hill	Dave Orton	Edward Whitaker
Gavin Beech	Pietro Innocenzi	Tom Park	Robbie Wilders
Richard Birch	Bruce Jackson	James Pyman	
James Burn	Paul Kealy	Graeme Rodway	Fashion: Ascot
Matt Butler	Patrick McCann	Stefan Searle	Racecourse and
Tom Collins	Keith Melrose	Tom Segal	Awon Golding
David Cramphorn	Kevin Morley	James Stevens	
Nick Freedman	Lee Mottershead	Shane Tetley	
Jonathan Harding	Julian Muscat	Craig Thake	

With grateful thanks to Ascot Racecourse for their invaluable assistance

Published in 2019 by Racing Post Books
27 Kingfisher Court, Hambridge Road, Newbury, RG14 5SJ

ISBN 978-1-83950-008-4
Printed in Great Britain by Buxton Press Limited

Welcome to the Racing Post's Royal Ascot Guide for 2019, which has 208 pages packed with all the information and insight you need to get prepared for the most spectacular five days in the world of racing.

Just like Royal Ascot itself, this guide offers a mix of everything – a close-up look at the best horses, trainers and jockeys, plus the pageantry, fashion, food and drink that make this a race meeting like no other. The guide features an in-depth look at all 30 races across the five days, accompanied by tips, betting pointers and analysis to help you find those all-important winners.

Along with profiles of the leading horses in a section stretching to more than 60 pages, we also have the lowdown on the top trainers and jockeys – all with handy tips on how to make money following them at Royal Ascot.

The draw, the handicaps, the trends and the international challenge are also considered by the Racing Post's team of experts as they weigh up the factors that make the difference at Flat racing's most prestigious and competitive fixture.

Nick Pulford
Editor

28

104

12

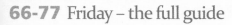

120

30

THIS IS ROYAL ASCOT

Julian Muscat looks forward to five magical days in June

Nothing else comes close. Travel the world and you won't find five consecutive days of racing to match the thrill of Royal Ascot.

Combine the superb quality of the racing with high-end fashion and a garden-party atmosphere and you have a race meeting in a realm of its own.

That's why more than 300,000 spectators make the annual visit. That's why America's coast-to-coast broadcaster, NBC, devotes more than four hours of live coverage to Royal Ascot every day.

And that's why more than 170 other countries also tune in.

The racing is a massive draw, of course. With eight Group 1 contests, including the first three in a magical burst on opening day, the quality of the sport is unsurpassed.

Seven of the top ten European-based horses of 2018 – based on world rankings – ran at last year's royal meeting and sprinters from Australia are a regular feature, as are runners from Wesley Ward's American stable.

This eclectic equine gathering makes Royal Ascot Britain's only truly global racing festival. But that's just for starters.

Packed trackside vantage points and viewing steps around the parade ring attest to the popularity of the royal family as horse-drawn carriages convey the Queen and guests from Windsor Great Park down the straight mile before the start of racing each day.

Along with the pageantry, there's the soul-warming sight of racegoers dressed appropriately for an informal royal gathering.

The more outlandish outfits grab the headlines but for most racegoers it's about dressing up for a big day out and having fun.

The Royal Enclosure may remain a symbol of Britain's social order but this is more than offset by the fact that every other enclosure is at least as good.

Ascot is one place where the quality of facilities is exemplary right across the racecourse and the sense of being at a big party gives the royal meeting an atmosphere all of its own, not least at the communal singsong at the end of each day.

With luck, the weather will be kind and you might have a winner or two as well.

ROYAL ASCOT ESSENTIALS

DATES

- Royal Ascot 2019 takes place over five days from Tuesday June 18 to Saturday June 22

TICKETS

- **Royal Enclosure** Available only to members and their guests, or non-members with a hospitality guest day badge
- **Queen Anne Enclosure** £77 Tue & Wed, £90 Thu-Sat
- **Village Enclosure** £69 Thu & Fri, £71 Sat
- **Windsor Enclosure** £37 Tue & Wed, £46 Thu-Sat

BY CAR

- **From London & the North** M4 Junction 6 onto the A332 Windsor bypass and follow the signs to Ascot
- **From the West** M4 Junction 10 to the A329(M) signed to Bracknell and follow the signs to Ascot
- **From the South & East** M3 Junction 3 onto the A332 signed

RACING POST

- Everything you need for Royal Ascot – web, app and newspaper
- Unrivalled cards, form, previews and tips
- Guiding you through all the action in our daily Postcasts
- Replays, results and analysis
- Stay up to date with all the news and colour from the track every day
- Live Tipster with up-to-the-minute punting news and insight
- Alastair Down heads the best reporting team in the business

to Bracknell and follow the signs to Ascot

- **From the Midlands** M40 southbound, Junction 4. Take the A404 towards the M4 (Junction 8/9). On the M4 head towards Heathrow/London. Leave M4 at Junction 6 and follow the A332 Windsor bypass to Ascot

- More than 8,000 car parking spaces are available and pre-booking is advised. Car Park 8 costs £40 per day

BY TRAIN

- South West Trains runs a frequent service to Ascot from Reading, Guildford and London Waterloo. The average journey time is 27 minutes from Reading and 52 minutes from Waterloo. Ascot's railway station is a seven-minute walk from the racecourse

TV DETAILS

- All 30 races will be broadcast live on ITV, totalling around 30 hours of live coverage across the week
- The Opening Show preview programme will be shown daily at 9am on ITV4 (9.30am on Saturday) and coverage of the racing will start at 1.30pm
- Sky Sports Racing will also broadcast live from Ascot for each of the five days

Ladbrokes
WHERE THE NATION PLAYS

ROYAL ASCOT
NEW CUSTOMER OFFER

PIP THIS TO THE POST!

Bet £5 get £20 in free bets using promo code: 20FREE

Available online & mobile

20
5

DOWNLOAD THE APP

A DAY AT ROYAL ASCOT
Top-class racing and so much more

2PM

The royal procession starts at the top of the course, passing each of the enclosures during its journey along the straight mile. Each landau carriage carries four people, with the Queen at the head of the group. As the carriages reach the grandstand, the national anthem is played by a guards band and the procession ends with a grand entrance to the parade ring

10.30AM

The famous Greencoats open the gates to signal the start of the day. Early arrivals can enjoy breakfast and take in the sights, such as the impressive bronze statues of the royal family, before finding a spot for lunch

2.30PM

Racing gets under way at the same time every day, continuing the tradition of majestic sport on the heath stretching back more than 300 years. The best of the opening races is undoubtedly the Queen Anne Stakes, the stupendous Tuesday curtain-raiser, with the other four days all starting with two-year-old races

5.35PM

The scheduled start time for the last of the six races each day, bringing to an end more than three hours of top-class action

6PM

Every day at Royal Ascot is rounded off with a session of communal singing at the Bandstand, a tradition that has been going since the 1970s. Racegoers join in with a choir led by the Royal Welsh Guards to run through a songbook ranging from patriotic ballads such as Land of Hope and Glory to modern classics like Neil Diamond's Sweet Caroline

8PM/9PM

Racegoers can enjoy a summer's evening before the day draws to a close at 8pm in the Royal, Queen

Anne and Windsor Enclosures, while on Thursday, Friday and Saturday the party in the Village Enclosure continues until 9pm with bands and DJs

THE ENCLOSURES

ROYAL ENCLOSURE

The most exclusive area with the best views from the grandstand and by the winning post. Membership for the Royal Enclosure is by invitation only and members can book badges for themselves and their guests (day badges start at £120). A formal dress code applies, including full morning suit for gentlemen

QUEEN ANNE ENCLOSURE

The premier public area at Royal Ascot, providing access to the pre-parade ring, winner's enclosure and parade ring and to facilities and viewing areas on the concourse level of the grandstand. Ladies are required to wear a hat and gentlemen a matching suit and a tie. £77 Tue & Wed, £90 Thu-Sat

VILLAGE ENCLOSURE

Situated on the infield on the opposite side of the track from the grandstand, this was introduced in 2017 and operates on Thursday to Saturday. The aim is to create a party atmosphere with live music from 11am to 8pm or 9pm, champagne and cocktail bars and eating options from boutique restaurants to street food. The dress code is less formal than in the Queen Anne Enclosure and the advice is to dress for the outdoors. Ladies are required to wear a hat and gentlemen a suit and tie. £69 Thu & Fri, £71 Sat

WINDSOR ENCLOSURE

This area is located furthest up the course from the winning post and no formal dress code applies, although racegoers are encouraged to dress for the occasion. There is a range of food stalls, champagne and Pimm's bars, with live music or DJ until 7pm. Picnics are welcome subject to Ascot's picnic policy. £37 Tue & Wed, £46 Thu-Sat

PICNICS

*I*f you are planning on bringing your own picnic, these are permitted in the Windsor and Heath Enclosures only. They must be carried in a picnic hamper or cool bag/box and sharp-bladed kitchen knives are not permitted. Each customer (over the age of 18) is allowed to bring one bottle of sparkling wine or champagne to accompany their picnic (no other type of alcoholic drink can be brought in).

Blankets and fold-up chairs are permitted and private picnic benches, seating six, can be pre-booked in the Windsor Enclosure at a cost of £180.

Royal Enclosure, Queen Anne Enclosure and Village Enclosure guests who bring their own can picnic only in the car and coach parks. No food, drinks or snacks can be taken into the Royal, Queen Anne or Village Enclosures.

A range of picnics can be pre-ordered, priced from £90 for Queen Anne and Village Enclosure guests and from £60 for the Windsor Enclosure.

Fortnum & Mason provide the picnics for the Queen Anne and Village Enclosures, with a Fortnum's Feast priced at £150 for two. Presented in a wicker basket, this includes a bottle of English sparkling wine along with cutlery, plates, glasses and a salt and pepper cruet set. A simpler Fortnum's picnic with wine is £95, presented in a reusable cool bag and again with cutlery etc.

An afternoon tea picnic for two is also available in the Queen Anne and Village Enclosures, including a range of sandwiches, luxury fruit scones and cakes, and a 375ml bottle

ROYAL ASCOT

THE FORTNUM'S FEAST

A selection of classic British picnic favourites curated by the famed
Fortnum & Mason, complete with a bottle of Fortnum's English Sparkling Wine.
Serving two people, the picnic is housed in an iconic Fortnum's wicker basket
which includes cutlery, plates, glasses and a salt & pepper cruet set.

Chicken liver parfait with shallot, cornichon & port jelly with crispbreads
Contains wheat (gluten), milk, eggs, sulphites

Rare roasted sirloin of beef with Tewkesbury mustard, potato & chive salad
Contains mustard, sulphites

Prawn & lobster cocktail
Contains barley (gluten), eggs, fish, crustaceans, molluscs, celery

Truffled Pecorino & farfalle salad with rocket pesto
Contains wheat (gluten), milk

Heritage tomato & basil oil salad
Contains mustard, celery

Asparagus & goat cheese tart
Contains wheat (gluten), milk, eggs, lupin

Mixed leaf salad with lemon vinaigrette

British cheese plate, pickle, grapes & crackers
Contains wheat (gluten), milk, celery

Chocolate trifle with glacé fruits
Contains nuts (almonds), milk, egg, soya, sulphites

Served with Fortnum's English Sparkling Wine, Camel Valley / 750ml bottle
Contains sulphites

THE FORTNUM'S FEAST WITH SPARKLING WINE - £150

IDEAL FOR TWO PEOPLE
Please consume on day of purchase.

FORTNUM & MASON
EST 1707

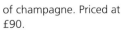

of champagne. Priced at £90.

In the Windsor Enclosure a picnic for two is £60 (£80 with Prosecco) or £195 for eight people (£275 with Prosecco).

DAY ONE

Royal Ascot's five-day feast starts with three mouthwatering Group 1 events in the first four races.

Only British Champions Day at Ascot in October can top three elite races on the same card and the royal meeting roars to life with the Queen Anne Stakes, a Group 1 race for four-year-olds and upwards over the straight mile.

This is one of the most international races, with winners from four different countries in the past six years, and often the first step towards champion miler honours.

The second Group 1 is the King's Stand Stakes, which is all about sizzling pace as the best five-furlong sprinters zip down the straight course in less than a minute.

This also has an international roll of honour, featuring winners from Australia and Hong Kong, and often produces a tight finish.

The Classic miling colts – many of whom will be coming from Guineas assignments in Britain, Ireland and France – traditionally clash in the St James's Palace Stakes, the third Group 1.

Whereas the Queen Anne is run on the straight mile, this contest races around the bend, putting the emphasis on a jockey possessing excellent race positioning as well as a mount with a superior turn of foot. Among the greats who have passed the test are Brigadier Gerard (1971), Kris

(1979), Frankel (2011) and Kingman (2014).

Also on the menu is the Group 2 Coventry Stakes, renowned as the premier race for two-year-old colts at the meeting and often the first showcase for a top-class performer. Four winners since 2007 went on to Classic success the following year in the 2,000 Guineas at Newmarket or the Irish 2,000 Guineas.

The emphasis turns to stamina for the Ascot Stakes, a handicap run over the marathon trip of two and a half miles. This contest allows the top jumps trainers to shine at Flat racing's most prestigious meeting and none more so than multiple Irish champion Willie Mullins, who had the first, third, fourth and fifth last year.

The Listed Wolferton Stakes, run over a mile and a quarter for four-year-olds and upwards, completes a stunning first-day programme. The balance swings back to the top Flat trainers here, with British champion John Gosden having taken four of the last eight runnings.

Tuesday June 18

RUNNING ORDER

2.30 Queen Anne Stakes (Group 1)   **1m** 4yo+   £600,000
Last year's winner: Accidental Agent 33-1

3.05 Coventry Stakes (Group 2)   **6f** 2yo   £150,000
Last year's winner: Calyx 2-1f (below)

3.40 King's Stand Stakes (Group 1)   **5f** 3yo+   £500,000
Last year's winner: Blue Point 6-1

4.20 St James's Palace Stakes (Group 1)   **1m** 3yo colts   £500,000
Last year's winner: Without Parole 9-4f

5.00 Ascot Stakes (Handicap)   **2m4f** 4yo+   £90,000
Last year's winner: Lagostovegas 10-1

5.35 Wolferton Stakes (Listed)   **1m2f** 4yo+   £100,000
Last year's winner: Monarchs Glen 8-1

Race value is total prize-money

THIS is the meeting's top mile race for older horses (aged four and up) and usually goes to an established star but last year there was a big upset when 33-1 shot Accidental Agent scored an emotional success for Eve Johnson Houghton. Close behind in a blanket finish were Lord Glitters (20-1), Lightning Spear (10-1) and Century Dream (20-1), while the first three in the betting all finished outside the first six.

Accidental Agent equalled the record for the longest-priced winner (Berrilldon was also 33-1 in 1912, when the race was known by its original name, the Trial Stakes) and was the first from outside the top four in the betting to land the prize since Refuse To Bend (12-1) in 2004. The longest-priced

winner in the intervening period was Declaration Of War (15-2) in 2013.

A couple of less surprising aspects of Accidental Agent's win were that he was the 14th four-year-old to land the race in 19 runnings since 2000 (all the others were five) and had prepped in the Lockinge – the last eight British-trained winners of the Queen Anne had run in the Newbury Group 1 (finishing 82411116).

Aidan O'Brien's last two winners also prepped in the Lockinge (finishing 65) and the US-trained Tepin in 2016 is the only one of the last 12 winners who had not run in a Group 1 last time (a Grade 2 at Churchill Downs in her case) – the three French-trained winners had all run in the Prix d'Ispahan.

Eight of the last ten winners came into the race

with an adjusted Racing Post Rating of at least 138 and already with Group 1 success on their record. The

Story of the last ten years

	FORM	WINNER	AGE	& WGT	Adj RPR	SP	TRAINER	BEST RPR LAST 12 MONTHS (RUNS SINCE)
18	48-36	**Accidental Agent** C	4	9-0	127^{-10}	33-1	Eve Johnson Houghton	won Ascot Class 2 hcap (7f) (4)
17	12-31	**Ribchester** C, D	4	9-0	139^T	11-10f	Richard Fahey	won Lockinge Stakes Gp1 (1m) (0)
16	-1111	**Tepin** D	5	8-11	138^T	11-2	Mark Casse (USA)	won Keeneland Gd1 (1m½f) (1)
15	1-111	**Solow** D	5	9-0	139^{-2}	11-8f	Freddy Head (FR)	won Dubai Turf Gp1 (1m1f) (1)
14	4216-	**Toronado** C, D	4	9-0	143^T	4-5f	Richard Hannon	won Sussex Stakes Gp1 (1m) (1)
13	11-15	**Declaration Of War** D, BF	4	9-0	128^{-11}	15-2	Aidan O'Brien (IRE)	won Leopardstown Listed (1m) (1)
12	111-1	**Frankel** D	4	9-0	153^T	1-10f	Sir Henry Cecil	won Lockinge Stakes Gp1 (1m) (0)
11	111-1	**Canford Cliffs** C, D	4	9-0	144^T	11-8	Richard Hannon snr	won Sussex Stakes Gp1 (1m) (1)
10	131-1	**Goldikova** D	5	8-11	148^T	11-8f	Freddy Head (FR)	won Prix Jacques le Marois Gp1 (1m) (3)
09	1-814	**Paco Boy** D, BF	4	9-0	141^{-2}	10-3	Richard Hannon snr	won Prix de la Foret Gp1 (7f) (3)

WINS-PL-RUNS 4yo 7-9-50, 5yo 3-6-36, 6yo+ 0-4-26 **FAVOURITES** -£0.25

TRAINERS IN THIS RACE (w-pl-r) Freddy Head 2-2-5, Aidan O'Brien 1-4-12, Richard Hannon 1-0-8, Eve Johnson Houghton 1-0-1, Andre Fabre 0-1-2, Andrew Balding 0-2-7, David O'Meara 0-1-6, John Gosden 0-1-2, William Haggas 0-2-2, Roger Varian 0-2-4

FATE OF FAVOURITES 6121011210 **POSITION OF WINNER IN MARKET** 2121211310

2.30 Queen Anne Stakes

Accidental Agent (orange cap) speeds home to land last year's Queen Anne Stakes at 33-1 under Charlie Bishop

Key trends
▶ *Aged four or five, ten winners in ten runnings*
▶ *Distance winner, 9/10*
▶ *Ran earlier that year, 9/10 (eight had won)*
▶ *Adjusted Racing Post Rating of at least 138, 8/10*
▶ *Rated within 2lb of RPR top-rated, 8/10 (six were top-rated)*
▶ *Group 1 winner, 8/10*

Other factors
▶ *Three winners were trained by the Hannon yard. Three of the other seven were trained in France or America*
▶ *Six winners had run in the Lockinge, in which they finished 411516; seven Lockinge winners ran, finishing 2115219*

Roll of honour

Longest-priced winner
Accidental Agent 33-1 (2018)

Shortest-priced winner
Frankel 1-10 (2012)

Most successful trainer
7 wins: **Saeed Bin Suroor**
Charnwood Forest (1996), Allied Forces (1997), Intikhab (1998), Cape Cross (1999), Dubai Destination (2003), Refuse To Bend (2004), Ramonti (2007)

Most successful jockey
6 wins: **Frankie Dettori**
Markofdistinction (1990), Allied Forces (1997), Intikhab (1998), Dubai Destination (2003), Refuse To Bend (2004), Ramonti (2007)

Most successful owner
8 wins: **Godolphin**
Charnwood Forest (1996), Allied Forces (1997), Intikhab (1998), Cape Cross (1999), Dubai Destination (2003), Refuse To Bend (2004), Ramonti (2007), Ribchester (2017)

*All figures since 1946

exceptions to that rule in both cases were Accidental Agent and Declaration Of War – he had run in a Group 1 last time (fifth in the Lockinge) but was yet to win above Group 3 level.

Often the previous year's Guineas and Royal Ascot results are a good sign of the right quality. Half of the 14 four-year-old winners since 2000 had secured a top-three finish in a Guineas (three won) or in the St James's Palace Stakes (two won). Most of the other four-year-old winners were late developers or had been held up by injury the previous year.

Saeed Bin Suroor is the leading trainer with seven winners but the last of them was Ramonti in 2007 and he had the beaten favourite, Benbatl (11-4), last year.

In recent years more significant yards have been Ballydoyle and the Hannon stable. Since 2008 with fancied runners (below 10-1) the form figures for O'Brien are 1662129 and for the Hannons they are 121154.

The recent French record is good, with three wins and five places from 16 runners since 2005.

3.05 Coventry Stakes

THIS is the most valuable race for juveniles at Royal Ascot and the season's first high-class contest for the age group, regularly proving a stepping stone to Group 1 level later in the year.

Unfortunately last year's winner, Calyx, was unable to run again as a juvenile but runner-up Advertise did go on to Group 1 success in the Phoenix Stakes.

One run is often enough to prepare for this test, as it was for Calyx and nine others in the past 20 years (only three winners in that period had run more than twice).

All of those once-raced juveniles had won, and indeed just four of the last 20 winners had suffered a defeat before Ascot. The last winner to arrive off the back of a last-time-out defeat

Key trends
▶ *Lost maiden tag, 10/10*
▶ *Won last time out, 10/10*
▶ *Rated within 4lb of RPR top-rated, 8/10 (six were top-rated)*
▶ *Adjusted RPR of at least 110, 8/10*
▶ *Won a previous start by at least two lengths, 8/10*
▶ *Distance winner, 8/10*
▶ *By a sire with a stamina index between 7.1f and 9.9f, 6/10*

Other factors
▶ *Nine winners came here undefeated. Buratino, who won in 2015, had been beaten twice over 5f but was undefeated over 6f*
▶ *Rajasinghe returned 11-1 in 2017 while War Command obliged at 20-1 in 2013, but the other eight winners started in single figures, including six favourites (one joint)*

was Harbour Master in 1997.

Just four of the last 20 winners had scored only at 5f, which points to winning form over 6f (or even 7f) being important in preparation for Ascot's stiff test. Key races to check out are the National Stakes at Sandown, the Woodcote Stakes at Epsom, the Marble Hill Stakes at the Curragh, Gowran Park 7f races and Newbury May maidens. It is also worth noting that three of the last four winners started their careers on the all-weather.

Market position is a good guide, with 12 of the last 20 winners having been first or second favourite and only three of those 20 priced above 8-1 (two were 20-1 shots trained by Aidan O'Brien, the top trainer in the race with eight victories).

Story of the last ten years

FORM	WINNER	AGE & WGT	Adj RPR	SP	TRAINER	BEST RPR LAST 12 MONTHS (RUNS SINCE)
18 1	**Calyx** D	2 9-1	115-2	2-1f	John Gosden	won Newmarket Class 4 nov (6f) (0)
17 1	**Rajasinghe** D	2 9-1	103-13	11-1	Richard Spencer	won Newcastle Class 4 nov (6f) (0)
16 11	**Caravaggio**	2 9-1	119T	13-8f	Aidan O'Brien (IRE)	won Curragh Listed (5f) (0)
15 13121	**Buratino** D	2 9-1	118T	6-1	Mark Johnston	won Woodcote Stakes Listed (6f) (0)
14 1	**The Wow Signal** D	2 9-1	110-4	5-1j	John Quinn	won Ayr Class 4 mdn (6f) (0)
13 1	**War Command**	2 9-1	104-12	20-1	Aidan O'Brien (IRE)	won Leopardstown mdn (7f) (0)
12 111	**Dawn Approach** D	2 9-1	118T	7-2	Jim Bolger (IRE)	won Naas Listed (6f) (0)
11 11	**Power** D	2 9-1	117T	4-1f	Aidan O'Brien (IRE)	won Curragh Listed (5f) (0)
10 1	**Strong Suit** D	2 9-1	113T	15-8f	Richard Hannon snr	won Newbury Class 4 mdn (6f) (0)
09 1	**Canford Cliffs** D	2 9-1	112-T	7-4f	Richard Hannon snr	won Newbury Class 4 mdn (6f) (0)

FAVOURITES £6.25 **TRAINERS IN THIS RACE** (w-pl-r) Aidan O'Brien 3-5-16, Mark Johnston 1-1-13, John Gosden 1-0-2, Brian Meehan 0-2-7, Charlie Hills 0-0-7, Charlie Appleby 0-0-3, Clive Cox 0-1-5, Richard Hannon 0-2-8, Wesley Ward 0-0-3, William Haggas 0-1-3
FATE OF FAVOURITES 1114610141 **POSITION OF WINNER IN MARKET** 1112913161

BEST PRICE GUARANTEED
➤ ALL ◀
ROYAL ASCOT RACES

**AVAILABLE ONLINE, MOBILE AND IN-SHOP
WITH YOUR CONNECT CARD**

The smart money's on *CORAL*

DAY ONE

THIS is the fastest race of the week, usually completed in less than a minute, and was perfect for the Australian speedsters who led the first wave of international challengers in the noughties. Four of the seven runnings from 2003 to 2009 went to Australia but their success has ebbed and seven of the last nine have gone to Britain or Ireland, with Hong Kong (Little Bridge in 2012) and the United States (Lady Aurelia in 2017) providing the most recent winners from outside Europe.

Six of those last seven winners from Britain and Ireland had contested the Palace House Stakes at Newmarket or the Temple Stakes at Haydock (and frequently both) that season and five of them had won at least one of those contests (the other was third) – a win in the Palace House seems to count for more, with five of the last nine to attempt the double having been successful (compared with only one of the last nine Temple winners to try).

Last year Temple winner Battaash was runner-up here and Palace House winner

Story of the last ten years

FORM	WINNER	AGE	& WGT	Adj RPR	SP	TRAINER	BEST RPR LAST 12 MONTHS (RUNS SINCE)
18 41-29	**Blue Point** C	4	9-4	131^{-7}	6-1	Charlie Appleby	2nd Meydan Gp2 (5f) (1)
17 113-1	**Lady Aurelia** CD	3	8-9	138^T	7-2	Wesley Ward (USA)	won Keeneland Listed (5½f) (0)
16 05-11	**Profitable** D	4	9-4	131^{-3}	4-1	Clive Cox	won Temple Stakes Gp2 (5f) (0)
15 42-17	**Goldream** CD	6	9-4	125^{-6}	20-1	Robert Cowell	won Palace House Stakes Gp3 (5f) (1)
14 2-471	**Sole Power** CD	7	9-4	130^T	5-1	Eddie Lynam (IRE)	won King's Stand Stakes Gp1 (5f) (7)
13 -2414	**Sole Power** D, BF	6	9-4	127^{-6}	8-1	Eddie Lynam (IRE)	won Palace House Stakes Gp3 (5f) (1)
12 -7611	**Little Bridge** D	6	9-4	132^{-1}	12-1	Danny Shum (HK)	won Sha Tin Listed hcap (5f) (1)
11 59432	**Prohibit** CD	6	9-4	126^{-6}	7-1	Robert Cowell	2nd Prix du Gros-Chene Gp2 (5f) (0)
10 0-112	**Equiano** CD, BF	5	9-4	129^{-4}	9-2	Barry Hills	2nd Temple Stakes Gp2 (5f) (0)
09 -2151	**Scenic Blast** D	5	9-4	131^T	11-4f	Daniel Morton (AUS)	won Flemington Gd1 hcap (6f) (0)

WINS-PL-RUNS 3yo 1-2-23, 4yo 2-8-49, 5yo 2-5-34, 6yo+ 5-5-63 **FAVOURITES** -£6.25

TRAINERS IN THIS RACE (w-pl-r) Charlie Appleby 1-0-3, Wesley Ward 1-0-4, Aidan O'Brien 0-0-6, Charlie Hills 0-2-4, David Griffiths 0-0-5, Jeremy Noseda 0-1-1, Kevin Ryan 0-2-6, William Haggas 0-1-4

FATE OF FAVOURITES 1660235030 **POSITION OF WINNER IN MARKET** 1345438223

3.40 King's Stand Stakes

William Buick roars to the crowd as Blue Point wins the 2018 King's Stand in fine style

Mabs Cross was third (the latter went on to Group 1 success later in the season) and unusually Blue Point, the winner, came off a spring campaign in Dubai and Hong Kong (where he had been last of nine in a Group 1 on his latest outing).

Significant races from further afield are the Prix du Gros-Chene (The Tatling in 2004, Equiano in 2008 and Prohibit in 2011 all placed before coming here) and the Prix de Saint-Georges, won by French-trained Chineur before his King's Stand victory in 2005 (Prohibit fourth in 2011).

Group 1-winning form is important with overseas raiders (all four Australian winners and Lady Aurelia

qualified, with Hong Kong's Little Bridge an exception) but not so much for the British and Irish (four of the last seven were scoring for the first time at this level). A good level of Group form is virtually a must, however.

Favourites can be found out (only two of the last 24 have won) but the market is still a good guide. Since Choisir's 25-1 success in 2003, at a time when the Australian challenge was underestimated, 12 of the 15 winners have been no bigger than 8-1 and nine of those came from the top three in the betting.

Key trends
▶ *Adjusted RPR of at least 125, 10/10*
▶ *Rated within 7lb of RPR top-rated, 10/10*
▶ *Ran at least twice that season, 9/10*
▶ *Won that season, 8/10*
▶ *Group winner over 5f, 7/10*
▶ *Drawn seven or higher, 8/10*

Other factors
▶ *There has been only one winning favourite in the past ten years*
▶ *Six beaten favourites had won a Group race last time (includes both joint-favourites from 2012)*
▶ *The record of Palace House winners is 010111133; Temple Stakes 2682034102*
▶ *International raiders have won three of the last ten, but Britain and Ireland have had seven of the last nine winners, five of whom ran in the Temple Stakes, finishing 23471*

Roll of honour
Longest-priced winners Squander Bug (1948) & Don't Worry Me (1997), 33-1

Shortest-priced winner Lochsong 3-10 (1994)

Most successful trainer
5 wins: **Vincent O'Brien**
Cassarate (1952), Abergwaun (1973), Godswalk (1977), Solinus (1978), Bluebird (1987)

Most successful jockey
7 wins: **Lester Piggott**
Right Boy (1957), Majority Rule (1963), Swing Easy (1971), Abergwaun (1973), Godswalk (1977), Solinus (1978), Never So Bold (1985)

*All figures since 1946

THIS is the third Group 1 of the opening day and last year's winner Without Parole was a rarity in that he had not run in a Guineas in Britain, Ireland and France, having instead made a rapid rise from a novice win in April followed by a Listed success in May.

He was only the second winner in 20 years not to have run in a Guineas, but the other one had run in a French Group 1 last time out (Most Improved was 14th in the French Derby in 2012).

Thirteen of the 18 who had run in a Guineas in the past two decades had enjoyed Classic success (some in more than one of them) and four more had been runner-up, with the worst position being Excellent Art's fourth in the French Guineas in 2007.

Key trends

- ▶ *Rated within 7lb of RPR top-rated, 10/10 (seven were top-rated)*
- ▶ *Had made the frame in a Group 1, 9/10*
- ▶ *Adjusted RPR of at least 130, 9/10*
- ▶ *From the first three in the market, 9/10*
- ▶ *Had finished in the first three in a 2,000 Guineas, 8/10*

Other factors

- ▶ *Winners who had run in a Guineas finished 53112112 at Newmarket and 11112 at the Curragh*
- ▶ *The last winner to run in the French Guineas was Excellent Art, who was fourth at Longchamp in 2007*
- ▶ *Last year, Without Parole became the first winner not to have run in a Group 1 that season since Shavian in 1990*
- ▶ *Aidan O'Brien has won seven of the last 19 runnings*

Three of the last nine St James's Palace winners – Canford Cliffs (2010), Kingman (2014) and Barney Roy (2017) – reversed form after a Guineas defeat at Newmarket. The first two of those had preceded Ascot success with Guineas victory in Ireland, while Barney Roy had not run in between.

Mastercraftsman in 2009 also reversed Newmarket form with the best performer from that Classic (winner Sea The Stars did not run at Ascot, having gone on to win the Derby instead).

Eleven of the last 20 winners had run in both the Newmarket and Irish Guineas and only two of those went backwards on the second run in terms of their finishing position (Zafeen was 14th in Ireland after being runner-up at Newmarket in 2003 and Galileo Gold went from first

4.20 St James's Palace Stakes

Without Parole lands the Listed Heron Stakes before going on to top-flight victory at Royal Ascot

Roll of honour

Longest-priced winner
Brief Truce 25-1 (1992)

Shortest-priced winner
Venture VII 1-33 (1960)

Most successful trainer
7 wins: **Aidan O'Brien**
Giant's Causeway (2000), Black Minnaloushe (2001), Rock Of Gibraltar (2002), Excellent Art (2007), Henrythenavigator (2008), Mastercraftsman (2009), Gleneagles (2015)

Most successful jockey
6 wins: **Mick Kinane**
Dara Monarch (1982), Brief Truce (1992), Grand Lodge (1994), Giant's Causeway (2000), Rock Of Gibraltar (2002), Azamour (2004)

Most successful owner
7 wins: **Coolmore partners**
Giant's Causeway (2000), Black Minnaloushe (2001), Rock Of Gibraltar (2002), Excellent Art (2007), Henrythenavigator (2008), Mastercraftsman (2009), Gleneagles (2015)

*All figures since 1946

to second). Of the seven who did not win at Newmarket, four stepped up to first place in Ireland.

Not surprisingly, given his tremendous strength in depth in the Classics division, Aidan O'Brien has won seven of the last 19 runnings. Between them, his seven winners had run in 13 Guineas with form figures of 2261114115111 – five of them had won a Guineas and three had done the Newmarket/Irish Guineas double.

The preponderance of strong Guineas form means favourites have a good record, with 13 winning in the past 20 years. No winner has been bigger than 9-1 in that period and the last shock winner was Brief Truce at 25-1 in 1992.

Story of the last ten years

FORM		WINNER	AGE	& WGT	Adj RPR	SP	TRAINER	BEST RPR LAST 12 MONTHS (RUNS SINCE)
18	1-11	**Without Parole** D	3	9-0	128-7	9-4f	John Gosden	won Yarmouth Class 5 nov (1m) **(1)**
17	1-12	**Barney Roy** C, D	3	9-0	132-7	5-2	Richard Hannon	2nd 2,000 Guineas Gp1 (1m) **(0)**
16	13-12	**Galileo Gold** D, BF	3	9-0	137T	6-1	Hugo Palmer	won 2,000 Guineas Gp1 (1m) **(1)**
15	11d-11	**Gleneagles** D	3	9-0	137T	8-15f	Aidan O'Brien (IRE)	won 2,000 Guineas Gp1 (1m) **(1)**
14	1-121	**Kingman** D	3	9-0	140T	8-11f	John Gosden	won Irish 2,000 Guineas Gp1 (1m) **(0)**
13	11-10	**Dawn Approach** C, D, BF	3	9-0	141T	5-4f	Jim Bolger (IRE)	won 2,000 Guineas Gp1 (1m) **(1)**
12	213-0	**Most Improved**	3	9-0	130-2	9-1	Brian Meehan	3rd Dewhurst Stakes Gp1 (7f) **(1)**
11	11-11	**Frankel** CD	3	9-0	147T	30-100f	Sir Henry Cecil	won 2,000 Guineas Gp1 (1m) **(0)**
10	3-231	**Canford Cliffs** C, D	3	9-0	140T	11-4j	Richard Hannon snr	won Irish 2,000 Guineas Gp1 (1m) **(0)**
09	14-51	**Mastercraftsman** D	3	9-0	136T	5-6f	Aidan O'Brien (IRE)	won Irish 2,000 Guineas Gp1 (1m) **(0)**

FAVOURITES £3.77 **TRAINERS IN THIS RACE (w-pl-r)** Aidan O'Brien 2-5-21, Richard Hannon 1-1-3, Hugo Palmer 1-0-2, Charlie Appleby 0-1-3, Saeed Bin Suroor 0-1-2

FATE OF FAVOURITES 1110111241 **POSITION OF WINNER IN MARKET** 1114111321

TRAINERS whose main emphasis is jump racing have come to dominate this long-distance contest, which is the first of four races at the meeting in which the field passes the winning post twice.

Irish-based handlers are responsible for six of the last seven winners, with Willie Mullins *(pictured)* claiming four of those successes – with Simenon in 2012, Clondaw Warrior in 2015, Thomas Hobson in 2017 and Lagostovegas last year. In fact, he had four of the first five in 2018 (from five runners), bringing his record since 2012 to 101770113450 from 12 runners for a level-stake profit of +19pt.

A favourite Mullins tactic is to attempt to double up in the Queen Alexandra Stakes (the final race on Saturday) – he did it with Simenon and just fell short with

Key trends

▶ *Raced no more than once on the Flat that season, 9/10*
▶ *Officially rated 85-95, 9/10*
▶ *Won a Flat handicap, 9/10 (exception was Group placed)*
▶ *Previously ran over hurdles, 9/10*
▶ *Won within last four Flat starts, 9/10 (exception had won last time out over hurdles)*
▶ *Carried between 9st and 9st 7lb, 7/10 (all three exceptions carried top weight of 9st 10lb)*

Other factors

▶ *Only two winners had scored beyond 2m on the Flat*

Thomas Hobson, who was second on the Saturday.

Other notable jumps trainers to win include Nicky Henderson, Jonjo O'Neill, David Pipe (and his

father Martin on four occasions) and Tony Martin (twice).

Another to watch is Alan King, who has strengthened his interest on the Flat in recent years. He had the sixth in this race last year and the third and fourth in 2017.

The last Newmarket trainer to win was Jane Chapple-Hyam with Judgethemoment in 2009 and before that it was Sir Michael Stoute with Cover Up in 2001.

Ten of the last 15 winners have been in a fairly narrow weights range from 8st 12lb to 9st 3lb, but a heavier burden is not a barrier to success with three winners and one runner-up carrying top weight of 9st 10lb in the seven runnings since 2012.

The market is a good guide, with eight of the last ten winners coming from the top four in the betting.

Story of the last ten years

FORM	WINNER	AGE & WGT	OR	SP	TRAINER	BEST RPR LAST 12 MONTHS (RUNS SINCE)
18 1332-	**Lagostovegas**	6 9-3	93-3	10-1	Willie Mullins (IRE)	2nd Naas Listed (1m4f) (0)
17 1211/	**Thomas Hobson**	7 9-10	100^T	4-1f	Willie Mullins (IRE)	Seasonal debut (0)
16 /21-1	**Jennies Jewel**	9 9-3	93-4	6-1	Jarlath Fahey (IRE)	won Curragh hcap (2m) (0)
15 2101-	**Clondaw Warrior**	8 9-0	89-4	5-1f	Willie Mullins (IRE)	won Leopardstown hcap (1m7f) (0)
14 120-0	**Domination**	7 9-7	92-3	12-1	Charles Byrnes (IRE)	2nd Galway hcap (2m) (2)
13 086/1	**Well Sharp**	5 9-10	95-6	9-1	Jonjo O'Neill	won York Class 3 hcap (2m½f) (0)
12 /350-	**Simenon**	5 9-10	95^T	8-1	Willie Mullins (IRE)	14th Newcastle Class 2 hcap (2m) (0)
11 /70-1	**Veiled**	5 9-3	88-1	11-2	Nicky Henderson	won Newmarket Class 4 hcap (1m6f) (0)
10 /131/	**Junior**	7 9-0	85^T	17-2	David Pipe	Seasonal debut (0)
09 66-11	**Judgethemoment** C	4 9-5	91-2	13-2	Jane Chapple-Hyam	won Ascot Class 3 hcap (2m) (0)

WINS-PL-RUNS 4yo 1-10-40, 5yo 3-11-68, 6yo+ 6-10-85 **FAVOURITES** £1.00
FATE OF FAVOURITES 0440251014 **POSITION OF WINNER IN MARKET** 2333471215

5.35 Wolferton Stakes

NAUGURATED in 2002 with the extension of Royal Ascot to a five-day meeting, this race was changed last year to become a 1m2f Listed conditions race for four-year-olds and older (rather than a handicap).

What did not change was that the race continued to be targeted by the top trainers for later-maturing, well-bred types. The first six last year came from championship-winning yards (two from John Gosden, two from Sir Michael Stoute and one each from Richard Hannon and Saeed Bin Suroor).

Gosden won with Monarchs Glen and was third with Muntahaa (his much lesser fancied runner) to cement his record as the most successful trainer in the race with four winners (all in the last eight runnings). Two common factors with his runners last year was that they had been tried in Group 1 company and had been gelded within the past year.

Seven of the past ten runnings have gone to Newmarket yards, with Stoute also on the scoreboard.

Aidan O'Brien is always likely to have the right type and he won with Sir Isaac Newton in 2016 when it was still a handicap.

Key trends
▶ *Aged four, 8/10*
▶ *Won at Class 3 level or higher, 8/10*
▶ *Ran no more than twice that season, 8/10*
▶ *Beaten on previous start, 8/10 (five over a different distance to this race)*
▶ *Drawn in single figures, 8/10*
▶ *Top-three finish last time out, 6/10 (one exception finished runner-up over hurdles last time)*

Other factors
▶ *John Gosden has won four times since 2011, including last year (Monarchs Glen) – the first time it was run as a conditions race rather than a handicap*

Monarchs Glen: scored last year when the Wolferton was run as a conditions race for the first time

Story of the last ten years

FORM	WINNER	AGE & WGT	Adj RPR	SP	TRAINER	BEST RPR LAST 12 MONTHS (RUNS SINCE)
18 211-0	**Monarchs Glen** D	4 9-8	123-3	8-1	John Gosden	won Newmarket Gp3 (1m1f) (1)
17 8-157	**Snoano** D	5 9-0	120-4	25-1	Tim Easterby	5th Chester Gp3 (1m2½f) (1)
16 64-23	**Sir Isaac Newton**	4 9-0	122T	7-1	Aidan O'Brien (IRE)	4th Leopardstown Gp2 (1m) (2)
15 1-11	**Mahsoob** D	4 9-3	124-1	7-4f	John Gosden	won York Class 2 hcap (1m2½f) (0)
14 24-13	**Contributer** D	4 9-5	116-6	9-1	Ed Dunlop	won Kempton Listed (1m2f) (0)
13 5750/	**Forgotten Voice** C	8 9-2	124T	12-1	Nicky Henderson	Seasonal debut (0)
12 14-11	**Gatewood** D	4 8-11	124T	3-1f	John Gosden	won Epsom Class 2 hcap (1m2f) (0)
11 1-523	**Beachfire** D, BF	4 8-9	123-2	12-1	John Gosden	3rd Goodwood Class 2 hcap (1m4f) (0)
10 111-2	**Rainbow Peak** CD, BF	4 9-4	124T	13-8f	Michael Jarvis	2nd Hambleton Stakes Listed hcap (1m) (0)
09 60-16	**Perfect Stride** C	4 9-5	122-5	8-1	Sir Michael Stoute	won Ascot Listed (1m) (1)

WINS-RUNS 4yo 8-13-65, 5yo 1-4-43, 6yo+ 1-4-37 **FAVOURITES** -£0.63

FATE OF FAVOURITES 0101521605 **POSITION OF WINNER IN MARKET** 3151741404

Swift Bet

on the RACING P●ST

Here's how it works

1 Log in and deposit to your betting accounts on all Racing Post products

2 Benefit from multiple bookmakers' promotions, including Best Odds Guaranteed

Ladbrokes *William* **HILL**
CORAL PADDYPOWER.
bet365 **betway**

3 Tap the odds buttons to add horses to your betslip

4 Place your bet, watch the race live and track your open bets on the Racing Post

FIVE OF THE BEST . . .

BACK THE BEST HORSE

That might sound overly simplistic but the point is that Royal Ascot is among the first of the big British meetings to be run at a truly conventional track. Many of the major form lines up to this point of the season have come from Newmarket, Chester or Epsom and they may not translate perfectly. Ascot has its specialists too, but it is essentially a fair track with a stiff finish, so put an additional emphasis on class when undertaking your form study.
Keith Melrose

FOLLOW THE LEADING SIRES

Pedigrees are worth a closer look at Royal Ascot than at any other Flat meeting. American-bred horses – particularly two-year-olds – by sires such as Scat Daddy and War Front flourish there, while Galileo and Dubawi have good records and Frankel was the leading sire at last year's meeting, with Sea The Stars and Shamardal two others who did well.
Tom Park

KEEP TABS ON FORM

Tackling the six juvenile races at Royal Ascot isn't easy but it's important to keep tabs on how the form works out from build-up races. If there is an easy winner and then a horse who was beaten several lengths comes out and wins next time, that adds substance to the winner's form. It is also worth being aware of which trainers are having a good season with their two-year-olds rather than assuming the usual big-hitters will come out on top.
David Baxter

Punting pointers

TAKE NOTES AT NEWBURY

Newbury's two-day Lockinge meeting is an informative staging post on the road to Royal Ascot. Races to note are the Lockinge as a Queen Anne prep, the London Gold Cup for Hampton Court Stakes contenders, the Carnarvon Stakes as a Commonwealth Cup prep and the various novice and maiden races, which often feature smart prospects from the bigger yards.
James Stevens

HIT THE PLAY BUTTON

Plenty of information can be gathered from form figures, collateral form and race comments, but it is just as important to watch as many replays as possible per horse in each race. With fewer pieces of form, this is most crucial in the two-year-old contests – my favourite and most profitable part of the royal meeting. Hype horses are often overbet in ante-post markets, leaving plenty of value for the more considered punter. When it comes to big handicaps and Group races, course form is the main starting point.
Tom Collins

FIVE SPECIAL TREATS

SIMON ROGAN

A lucky few in the Royal Enclosure may wish to find a place at Michelin four-star chef Simon Rogan's table-service restaurant, showcasing his innovative approach to seasonal produce found at his award-winning restaurants L'Enclume and Roganic. *From £104.50 per person; bookings sold out, some on-the-day availability; Royal Enclosure Gardens*

Simon Rogan at Royal Ascot

J SHEEKEY POP-UP

Royal Enclosure guests will be familiar with the timeless charm of Covent Garden seafood restaurant J Sheekey. Offering walk-up sittings, the restaurant brings highlights from its iconic menu to Royal Ascot, featuring the finest fish, shellfish and seasonal game. *Mains from £36; pre-booking not required, enquire on the day*

THE RESTAURANT IN THE VILLAGE

Revel in a boutique dining atmosphere like no other. Located within the Village Enclosure, this restaurant is vibrant, surprising, yet

unmistakably Royal Ascot and includes a four-course menu and spectacular 'Around the World' afternoon tea featuring sweet treats from 12 countries. *From £329 per person; limited availability*

AFTERNOON TEA

Racegoers can pre-book or walk-up on the day to sample afternoon tea by Master Pâtissier Eric Lanlard, proprietor of Cake Boy in London, whose mouthwatering creations include British strawberry tart royal, white chocolate and passion fruit eclair and violet and raspberry macarons. *From £38 per person, up to £57.50 for the Champagne afternoon tea; available at Windsor Greys (Royal Enclosure) and 1768 Grill & Tearooms (Queen Anne Enclosure)*

CHAMPAGNE

If you want to celebrate a winner, or just share a tipple with friends, a variety of bars serve Champagne, including the alfresco Maison 1743 by Moët & Chandon (serving Ascot's official Champagne) in the Queen Anne Enclosure.

DAY TWO

The Group 1 Prince of Wales's Stakes is the highlight of day two, and indeed of the entire week for many connoisseurs, and it is strange to think that it was revived only in 1968, a year before the current Prince of Wales's investiture.

At the same time the distance was reduced to a mile and a quarter and, having been upgraded to top-level-status in 2000, it is now firmly established as one of the world's best contests – last year it was officially Europe's top-ranked race at the distance. The grand roll of honour features luminaries such as Mtoto (1987 and 1988), Dubai Millennium (2000) and Ouija Board (2006).

Day two kicks off with the Group 2 Queen Mary Stakes, the meeting's premier race for two-year-old fillies. Blistering speed wins this five-furlong contest, with pocket rocket Lyric Fantasy (1992) and American star Lady Aurelia (2016) two of the outstanding winners.

The day now ends with another juvenile contest over

five furlongs, with the Listed Windsor Castle Stakes having been moved from last year's Saturday slot in a swap with the Jersey Stakes.

A different test is provided by the Queen's Vase, the day's longest race over a mile and three-quarters. This Group 2 contest for three-year-olds is often a showcase for a developing stayer, having been won by Stradivarius (last year's Gold Cup winner) and subsequent St Leger scorer Kew Gardens in the two runnings since the distance was reduced from two miles.

The third Group 2 race on the card is the Duke of Cambridge Stakes, run over the straight mile for fillies and mares aged four and upwards. Sir Michael Stoute, a dab hand with that type of horse, has had four winners since the race's inception in 2004.

The biggest field of the day will bring the spectacle of 30 runners thundering down the straight mile in the Royal Hunt Cup, one of the principal betting races of the week. A big plunge on a fancied horse is commonplace but this is always ferociously competitive and four of the last six winners went off at 16-1 or bigger.

Wednesday June 19

2.30 Queen Mary Stakes (Group 2) *Last year's winner: Signora Cabello 25-1*	**5f** 2yo fillies	£110,000
3.05 Queen's Vase (Group 2) *Last year's winner: Kew Gardens 100-30*	**1m6f** 3yo	£225,000
3.40 Duke of Cambridge Stakes (Group 2) *Last year's winner: Aljazzi 9-2*	**1m** 4yo+ fillies and mares	£175,000
4.20 Prince of Wales's Stakes (Group 1) *Last year's winner: Poet's Word 11-2*	**1m2f** 4yo+	£750,000
5.00 Royal Hunt Cup (Heritage Handicap) *Last year's winner: Settle For Bay 16-1*	**1m** 3yo+	£175,000
5.35 Windsor Castle Stakes (Listed) *Last year's winner: Soldier's Call 12-1*	**5f** 2yo	£90,000

Race value is total prize-money

THIS five-furlong dash is the premier race at the meeting restricted to two-year-old fillies – the only other of that ilk is the Albany Stakes, which is run over six furlongs on Friday and is a step lower than this Group 2.

The shape of the race has been influenced by US trainer Wesley Ward since he started to target Royal Ascot in 2009 and he has had three of the last ten winners as well as two beaten favourites (his last two winners also headed the market). His nine runners have finished 172401120, starting with Jealous Again's breakthrough success in 2009.

Other trainers noted for fast horses also appear on the roll of honour, including Richard Hannon snr, Mick Channon, Eddie Lynam and

Key trends

▶ *By a sire with stamina index between 5.9f and 8.4f, ten winners in last ten runnings*
▶ *Lost maiden tag, 9/10*
▶ *Adjusted Racing Post Rating of at least 102, 9/10*
▶ *Rated within 9lb of RPR top-rated, 8/10*
▶ *Won last time out, 8/10*
▶ *Distance winner, 7/10*
▶ *Ran at least twice, 6/10*

Other factors

▶ *Marygate Stakes winners at York have finished 2910801; Hilary Needler (Beverley) 0058200; National Stakes (Sandown) 012*
▶ *Two of the four winners to have had just one start were trained by Wesley Ward*
▶ *The three not to have won over the trip were all trained by Wesley Ward – two had won over 4½f and the other was still a maiden*

Clive Cox (along with Ward, they account for more than 40 per cent of the winners in the last quarter of a century).

This is less likely to go to one of the powerhouse stables, with just one winner for John Gosden and none for Aidan O'Brien or Godolphin duo Saeed Bin Suroor and Charlie Appleby.

High-class winning form is virtually essential (last year's winner, Signora Cabello, went off at 25-1 but was already a Listed winner in the Marygate Stakes at York, one of the more significant stepping stones).

Eight of the last ten winners had won last time out (both exceptions were trained by Ward) and four were unbeaten, while three of those who had been beaten had since bounced back with two straight wins.

Story of the last ten years

	FORM	WINNER		AGE & WGT	Adj RPR	SP	TRAINER	BEST RPR LAST 12 MONTHS (RUNS SINCE)
18	411	**Signora Cabello**	D	2 9-0	105-7	25-1	John Quinn	won York Listed (5f) (0)
17	1	**Heartache**	D	2 9-0	107-3	5-1	Clive Cox	won Bath Class 4 nov (5f) (0)
16	1	**Lady Aurelia**		2 9-0	112T	2-1f	Wesley Ward (USA)	won Keeneland (4½f) (0)
15	3	**Acapulco**	BF	2 9-0	91-15	5-2f	Wesley Ward (USA)	3rd Churchill Downs (4½f) (0)
14	61	**Anthem Alexander**	D	2 9-0	106-9	9-4f	Eddie Lynam (IRE)	won Tipperary mdn (5f) (0)
13	511	**Rizeena**	CD	2 8-12	112T	6-1	Clive Brittain	won Sandown Listed (5f) (0)
12	2411	**Ceiling Kitty**	D	2 8-12	106-8	20-1	Tom Dascombe	won York Listed (5f) (0)
11	11	**Best Terms**	D	2 8-12	104-11	12-1	Richard Hannon snr	won Newbury Class 3 (5f) (0)
10	1	**Maqaasid**	D	2 8-12	102-9	9-4f	John Gosden	won Sandown Class 4 mdn (5f) (0)
09	12	**Jealous Again**	BF	2 8-12	112-7	13-2	Wesley Ward (USA)	2nd Churchill Downs Gd3 (5f) (0)

FAVOURITES £3.00

TRAINERS IN THIS RACE (w-pl-r) Wesley Ward 3-2-9, Tom Dascombe 1-0-6, Aidan O'Brien 0-1-4, Brian Meehan 0-1-2, Clive Cox 1-1-5, Stan Moore 0-0-3, James Tate 0-0-2, Jeremy Noseda 0-0-1, Keith Dalgleish 0-1-4, Mark Johnston 0-0-8, Mick Channon 0-0-7, Richard Fahey 0-0-9, Richard Hannon 0-2-6, William Haggas 0-1-3, Ger Lyons 0-0-1

FATE OF FAVOURITES 4120011120 **POSITION OF WINNER IN MARKET** 5150311129

THIS 1m6f race, restricted to three-year-olds and designed to bring along future St Leger and Cup horses over staying trips, is in its third year over that distance and the reduction in trip from 2m may even have increased its influence. The 2017 winner Stradivarius came back to the royal meeting to land last year's Gold Cup in a dominant staying campaign, while last year's winner Kew Gardens went on to take the St Leger.

Whatever the distance, the race has been dominated by stables with the best resources for staying and middle-distance horses, with Mark Johnston (seven winners), Aidan O'Brien (six), Sir Michael Stoute (three), Saeed Bin Suroor (two) and John Gosden

(Run over 2m until 2017)

Key trends

▶ *Top-three finish last time out, 9/10*

▶ *By a sire with a stamina index in excess of 1m2f, 9/10*

▶ *Adjusted RPR of at least 112, 8/10*

▶ *Rated within 7lb of RPR top-rated, 8/10 (one exception was favourite but 21lb off top-rated)*

▶ *Won within last two starts, 6/10*

Other factors

▶ *Estimate in 2012 was the only winner to come straight from maiden company*

▶ *The only trainers to have won this since 2000 are Mark Johnston (seven times), Aidan O'Brien (six), Sir Michael Stoute (three), Saeed Bin Suroor (twice) and John Gosden (once)*

▶ *Six winners contested a Listed or Group race last time*

(one) the only active trainers to have been successful in the past two decades. O'Brien had the first three last year and Gosden was next best in fourth.

The market is often a good guide to the best prospects from the big stables, with nine of the last 11 winners coming from the top two in the betting. In that period, backing runners from those dominant stables that made the top two in the betting would have yielded a level-stakes profit of +18.03pt.

Kew Gardens had finished ninth behind Masar in the Derby before winning here and the reduction in distance might make this race increasingly attractive for those who have not quite made the grade in the middle-distance spring trials and Classics.

Story of the last ten years

	FORM	WINNER	AGE & WGT	Adj RPR	SP	TRAINER	BEST RPR LAST 12 MONTHS (RUNS SINCE)
18	1-329	**Kew Gardens**	3 9-0	121-7	10-3	Aidan O'Brien (IRE)	won Newmarket Listed (1m2f) (3)
17	41-12	**Stradivarius** BF	3 9-0	114-3	11-2	John Gosden	2nd Chester Class 3 hcap (1m4½f) (0)
16	3-213	**Sword Fighter**	3 9-3	99-16	33-1	Aidan O'Brien (IRE)	3rd Naas (1m4f) (0)
15	212-	**Aloft**	3 9-3	123T	5-2f	Aidan O'Brien (IRE)	2nd Racing Post Trophy Gp1 (1m) (0)
14	13-52	**Hartnell**	3 9-3	115T	7-2	Mark Johnston	2nd Lingfield Derby Trial Listed (1m3½f) (0)
13	41-11	**Leading Light**	3 9-4	121-T	5-4f	Aidan O'Brien (IRE)	won Gallinule Stakes Gp3 (1m2f) (0)
12	7-1	**Estimate**	3 8-12	98-21	3-1f	Sir Michael Stoute	won Salisbury Class 5 mdn (1m4f) (0)
11	45243	**Namibian**	3 9-1	121-T	7-2f	Mark Johnston	3rd Musselburgh Class 2 hcap (1m4½f) (0)
10	612-3	**Mikhail Glinka** BF	3 9-1	120-2	2-1f	Aidan O'Brien (IRE)	2nd Criterium de Saint-Cloud Gp1 (1m2f) (1)
09	11-13	**Holberg**	3 9-1	112-3	7-1	Mark Johnston	3rd Glasgow Stakes Listed (1m3f) (0)

FAVOURITES £7.25

TRAINERS IN THIS RACE (w-pl-r) Aidan O'Brien 5-5-17, Mark Johnston 3-1-17, John Gosden 1-2-8, Andrew Balding 0-1-6, Charlie Appleby 0-1-3, Dermot Weld 0-0-3, David Elsworth 0-0-3, David Simcock 0-0-2

FATE OF FAVOURITES 0111131440 **POSITION OF WINNER IN MARKET** 3111121022

DISCOVER

Shared Racehorse Ownership

Search for your perfect ownership experience at

inthepaddock.co.uk

THIS Group 2 contest for older fillies and mares is run over the straight mile, whereas the mile Group 1 for three-year-old fillies, Friday's Coronation Stakes, is held on the round course.

If there is one striking statistic from the relatively short history of this race, it is the appalling record of those who have had to carry a Group 1 penalty. In the 15 editions to date, 11 horses have lined up under such a penalty and all were beaten, with only Soviet Song in 2005 making the frame.

Part of the explanation for such a poor record among those asked to concede weight all round might be the race's role as a launch pad for the season, as four of those 11 with a Group 1 penalty had not had a

Key trends
▶ *Top-three finish that season, 10/10*
▶ *Had won a Group race, 10/10*
▶ *Adjusted RPR of at least 125, 9/10*
▶ *Rated within 6lb of RPR top-rated, 9/10*
▶ *Distance winner, 8/10*

Other factors
▶ *Winners of the Dahlia at Newmarket finished 2153941; the Chartwell at Lingfield 0205*
▶ *Seven fillies carrying the Group 1 penalty were beaten (6879558)*
▶ *Three had already won at Ascot, while two were Group placed at the previous year's Royal Ascot*

previous run that year. That contrasts starkly with the profile of the 15 winners, all but one of whom had run at least once that season.

It should be noted that the Group 1 penalty applies only to wins after August 31 the previous season and so having winning form at that level does not preclude a big performance here, as was demonstrated by the 2017 heroine Qemah, who had won the Coronation Stakes and Prix Rothschild in the summer of 2016.

High-class form is important, with four of the last seven winners having put up their best performance of the previous 12 months with a top-four finish in a Group 1 and the other three having done that with a top-three finish in a Group 2 (Aljazzi, last year's winner, had been second to Qemah in the 2017 edition of this race).

The Princess Elizabeth Stakes at Epsom has proved a useful stepping stone at a lower level.

Story of the last ten years

	FORM	WINNER	AGE & WGT	Adj RPR	SP	TRAINER	BEST RPR LAST 12 MONTHS (RUNS SINCE)
18	197-3	**Aljazzi** D	5 9-0	128^T	9-2	Marco Botti	won Sandown Gp3 (1m) (3)
17	113-2	**Qemah** C, D	4 9-0	131^T	5-2f	Jean-Claude Rouget (FR)	won Prix Rothschild Gp1 (1m) (2)
16	7-111	**Usherette** D	4 9-3	128^{-1}	9-4f	Andre Fabre (FR)	won Dahlia Stakes Gp2 (1m1f) (0)
15	00-33	**Amazing Maria**	4 9-0	119^{-9}	25-1	David O'Meara	3rd Lanwades Stud Stakes Gp2 (1m) (0)
14	712-2	**Integral** D, BF	4 9-0	130^T	9-4f	Sir Michael Stoute	2nd Sun Chariot Stakes Gp1 (1m) (1)
13	11d-1	**Duntle** CD	4 8-12	131^{-1}	10-3	David Wachman (IRE)	2nd Matron Stakes Gp1 (1m) (1)
12	647-2	**Joviality**	4 8-12	125^{-6}	11-1	John Gosden	4th Falmouth Stakes Gp1 (1m) (2)
11	-1122	**Lolly For Dolly** D, BF	4 8-12	127^{-4}	11-1	Tommy Stack (IRE)	won Gladness Stakes Gp3 (7f) (2)
10	114-1	**Strawberrydaiquiri** C, D	4 8-12	132^T	9-2	Sir Michael Stoute	won Sandown Listed (1m) (2)
09	144-3	**Spacious** D, BF	4 8-12	125^{-6}	10-1	James Fanshawe	4th Coronation Stakes Gp1 (1m) (4)

WINS-PL-RUNS 4yo 9-11-84, 5yo 1-7-23, 6yo+ 0-1-6 **FAVOURITES** £0.00

TRAINERS IN THIS RACE (w-pl-r) Sir Michael Stoute 2-2-8, Andre Fabre 1-1-4, Jean-Claude Rouget 1-0-1, James Fanshawe 1-2-5, Aidan O'Brien 0-0-2, Andrew Balding 0-1-3, Saeed Bin Suroor 0-2-7, Mick Channon 0-1-5

FATE OF FAVOURITES 6340615110 **POSITION OF WINNER IN MARKET** 5255215112

BRISTOL & BATH:
luxurychauffeurhirebristol.co.uk

BIRMINGHAM:
xurychauffeurhirebirmingham.co.uk

GLOUCESTERSHIRE & HEREFORDSHIRE:
jonnyrockschauffeurs.co.uk

OXFORDSHIRE:
luxurychauffeurhireoxford.co.uk

WILTSHIRE:
chauffeurhireswindon.co.uk

WORCESTERSHIRE:
luxurychauffeurhireworcester.co.uk

WARWICKSHIRE:
luxurychauffeurhirewarwick.co.uk

THIS is the top-ranked contest of Royal Ascot – based on the ratings of the first four finishers – and always one of the highlights of the European season at a mile and a quarter.

It is also one of the last chances for the cream of the older middle-distance crop to race one another on level terms before having to face the three-year-olds and their weight-for-age allowance.

Last year's race did not disappoint in terms of spectacle or quality, with Poet's Word (later the King George VI and Queen Elizabeth Stakes winner) scoring a big upset over Cracksman, who came back to his best in the autumn with another stunning win in the Champion Stakes to end up the world's top-rated

horse of 2018 alongside Australian wondermare Winx.

The typical winner has already proved top class, both in terms of races won and ratings achieved, and Poet's Word was something of a rarity in not having won at Group 1 level before. He was only the fourth such winner in the 19 runnings since the race was promoted to elite status in 2000, and it

is interesting to note that all four have struck in the last nine editions (the others being Byword, Free Eagle and My Dream Boat).

In terms of prep races that have a strong influence on the outcome, Britain is late in staging its first Group 1 of the season over the trip in comparison to Ireland and France, which means there have been a wide variety of successful routes.

Story of the last ten years

	FORM	WINNER	AGE	& WGT	Adj RPR	SP	TRAINER	BEST RPR LAST 12 MONTHS (RUNS SINCE)
18	26-21	**Poet's Word** D	5	9-0	134-11	11-2	Sir Michael Stoute	2nd Irish Champion Stakes Gp1 (1m2f) (4)
17	12-71	**Highland Reel** C, D	5	9-0	138-1	9-4	Aidan O'Brien (IRE)	2nd Prix de l'Arc de Triomphe Gp1 (1m4f) (4)
16	11-15	**My Dream Boat** D	4	9-0	134-11	16-1	Clive Cox	won Gordon Richards Stakes Gp3 (1m2f) (1)
15	2/13-	**Free Eagle** D	4	9-0	136-4	5-2f	Dermot Weld (IRE)	3rd Champion Stakes Gp1 (1m2f) (0)
14	122-0	**The Fugue** D	5	8-11	140-8	11-2	John Gosden	won Irish Champion Stakes Gp1 (1m2f) (3)
13	/1-11	**Al Kazeem** D	5	9-0	137T	11-4	Roger Charlton	won Tattersalls Gold Cup Gp1 (1m2½f) (0)
12	26-41	**So You Think** D	6	9-0	142T	4-5f	Aidan O'Brien (IRE)	won Eclipse Stakes Gp1 (1m2f) (6)
11	316-1	**Rewilding**	4	9-0	138-5	17-2	Mahmood Al Zarooni	won Dubai Sheema Classic Gp1 (1m4f) (0)
10	4-112	**Byword**	4	9-0	139T	5-2f	Andre Fabre (FR)	2nd Prix d'Ispahan Gp1 (1m1f) (0)
09	15-31	**Vision D'Etat** D	4	9-0	138-1	4-1	Eric Libaud (FR)	5th Prix de l'Arc de Triomphe Gp1 (1m4f) (2)

WINS-PL-RUNS 4yo 5-13-46, 5yo 4-3-28, 6yo+ 1-1-13 **FAVOURITES** -£1.20

TRAINERS IN THIS RACE (w-pl-r) Aidan O'Brien 2-3-11, Andre Fabre 1-0-1, John Gosden 1-4-11, Sir Michael Stoute 1-3-8, Andrew Balding 0-0-1, Charlie Appleby 0-0-3, David Simcock 0-0-2, Roger Varian 0-0-3, Saeed Bin Suroor 0-1-4, William Haggas 0-1-2

FATE OF FAVOURITES 2121431682 **POSITION OF WINNER IN MARKET** 3131221622

Poet's Word outguns Cracksman under James Doyle (below) in last year's Prince of Wales's

Since 2000 Poet's Word is the only one of the 17 winners who had already raced that season not to have posted his most recent outing at Group 1 level, although a trial to note at a lower level is the Group 3 Gordon Richards Stakes at Sandown (won by Al Kazeem in 2013 and My Dream Boat in 2016).

Another significant Group 3 is the Brigadier Gerard Stakes, also at Sandown, which was won by Poet's Word last year after his earlier good run in Group 1 company when second in the Dubai Sheema Classic at Meydan.

Horses coming off a break after a good performance on Dubai World Cup night also have a decent record, with The Fugue in 2014 the most recent of four such winners this century.

The Tattersalls Gold Cup has been the chosen warm-up for five winners during that period (among that number only Azamour in 2005 was beaten at the Curragh), while France's two early-season Group 1s, the Prix d'Ispahan and the Prix Ganay, have been a launch pad for three winners between them.

In a further sign that the cream rises to the top, only two of the 19 winners since 2000 were outside the top three in the betting.

41

THE Royal Ascot schedule now features a big handicap as the fifth race on each day and this is the first of the cavalry charges down the straight course, with 30 or more runners fanning out in the mile contest.

Margins are usually tight, with often no more than half a length in it at the line, but last year Settle For Bay scored by two and a quarter lengths – the biggest margin since the gambled-on Forgotten Voice won by the same distance in 2009.

David Marnane's Settle For Bay was the second Irish winner in the past three years following Portage's success for Michael Halford in 2017 that ended a 50-year drought for the raiding party.

Marnane became the latest different trainer to win the race in the last 11 runnings and the only current trainers

Key trends

▶ *Recorded a pre-race RPR of at least 99, 10/10*
▶ *Officially rated between 93 and 103, 9/10 (exception was penalised)*
▶ *Rated within 7lb of RPR top-rated, 9/10*
▶ *Won or placed in a field of at least 14 runners, 9/10*
▶ *Top-four finish at least once that season, 9/10 (exception was making reappearance)*
▶ *Carried between 8st 8lb and 9st 3lb, 9/10*
▶ *Aged four or five, 8/10*
▶ *Distance winner, 8/10*

Other factors

▶ *In 2016, Portage became the first winner under a penalty since Macadamia in 2003*
▶ *There have been only three winning favourites in the last 31 years*
▶ *Only two of the last ten winners were drawn in single figures; none was drawn between stalls 12 and 21*
▶ *Four winners wore some form of headgear*

with more than one success in the past quarter of a century are James Fanshawe (2003 and 2006) and John Gosden (2007 and 2015).

Extreme weight-carrying performances are difficult to achieve. Going back to the reopening of Ascot and its newly relaid track in 2006, no winner has been rated within 5lb of the topweight and only two winners have carried in excess of 9st 3lb.

Those at the top of the handicap can run well – seven horses carrying 9st 6lb or more have been placed in the past decade – but the last winner to defy such a weight was Governorship in 1988.

With only two winners having had a single-figure number cloth (both wore eight) and the lowest-rated being number 22 on the racecard over the 13 editions run at the new Ascot, the middle of the pack would appear to be the optimum.

Story of the last ten years

	FORM	WINNER	AGE	& WGT	OR	SP	TRAINER	BEST RPR LAST 12 MONTHS (RUNS SINCE)
18	11-14	**Settle For Bay** D	4	9-1	99-8	16-1	David Marnane (IRE)	4th Leopardstown hcap (7f) (0)
17	-4803	**Zhui Feng**	4	9-0	100-3	25-1	Amanda Perrett	4th Winter Derby Gp3 (1m2f) (3)
16	125-1	**Portage** (5ex) CD	4	9-5	105-7	10-1	Mick Halford (IRE)	5th Newmarket Class 2 hcap (1m1f) (1)
15	43-02	**Gm Hopkins** D, BF	4	9-3	103-2	8-1	John Gosden	2nd Newbury Class 2 hcap (1m) (0)
14	5950-	**Field Of Dream** C	7	9-1	101-1	20-1	Jamie Osborne	won Newmarket Class 2 hcap (7f) (4)
13	-0020	**Belgian Bill**	5	8-11	97-2	33-1	George Baker	won Kempton Class 2 hcap (7f) (6)
12	541-2	**Prince Of Johanne** D	6	9-3	100-1	16-1	Tom Tate	2nd York Listed hcap (1m) (0)
11	10-33	**Julienas** D, BF	4	8-8	93-2	12-1	Walter Swinburn	3rd Sandown Class 3 hcap (1m) (0)
10	19-44	**Invisible Man** D	4	8-9	95-7	28-1	Saeed Bin Suroor	won Pontefract Class 3 hcap (1m) (3)
09	1/11	**Forgotten Voice** D	4	9-1	101-3	4-1f	Jeremy Noseda	won Kempton Class 3 hcap (1m) (0)

WINS-PL-RUNS 4yo 7-14-121, 5yo 1-8-70, 6yo+ 2-8-94 **FAVOURITES** -£8.20

FATE OF FAVOURITES 1020000000 **POSITION OF WINNER IN MARKET** 1046082309

The world famous gentlemen's hatter, since 1898.

73 Jermyn Street • LONDON
252 Rue de Rivoli • PARIS

www.bates-hats.com

THIS Listed race over 5f for two-year-olds was moved from Tuesday to Saturday last year and has been switched again, slotting in here to allow the Jersey Stakes to move to a more prominent place on Saturday.

In recent years this has proved the juvenile race most open to a surprise result, with eight of the last 13 winners having been priced at 12-1 or bigger.

Perhaps the less high-profile stables save their best hopes for this contest, knowing that the big guns will aim their main fire at the more important juvenile races.

It is notable that eight trainers have achieved their first Royal Ascot success in the last 20 runnings of this contest, including Archie Watson with 12-1 shot

Key trends

▶ *Top-four finish last time out, 10/10 (six won)*
▶ *Lost maiden tag, 10/10*
▶ *By a sire with a stamina index of 6.5f-8f, 9/10*
▶ *Ran two or three times, 7/10 (all three exceptions were once-raced winners)*
▶ *Adjusted RPR of at least 94, 9/10 (exception was unrated US winner)*

Other factors

▶ *Only one winner had scored outside maiden/novice company (Frederick Engels in 2011)*
▶ *Fillies won five in a row between 1996 and 2000 but only two have been placed in the last ten years*
▶ *The race is often won by trainers not usually associated with having Royal Ascot winners*

Soldier's Call last year.

Even the major stables can produce a long-odds winner – Charlie Appleby at 16-1 in 2017 and John Gosden at 20-1 the year before that – and just four of the last ten winners came from the top six in the betting.

Aidan O'Brien's only success came with Washington DC in 2015 and this is a race that usually goes to a British-trained runner, although US trainer Wesley Ward has broken the mould twice with Strike The Tiger in 2009 (his breakthrough year at Royal Ascot) and Hootenanny in 2014.

Most winners had shown a decent level of form. The last ten had lost their maiden tag and the three once-raced winners in that period had all been successful, while three of the last five winners had already been tried in Listed company.

Story of the last ten years

	FORM	WINNER	AGE	& WGT	Adj RPR	SP	TRAINER	BEST RPR LAST 12 MONTHS (RUNS SINCE)
18	21	Soldeir's Call D	2	9-3	97-14	12-1	Archie Watson	won Haydock Class 4 nov (5f) (0)
17	14	Sound And Silence D	2	9-3	101-11	16-1	Charlie Appleby	4th Sandown Listed (5f) (0)
16	1	Ardad D	2	9-3	94-14	20-1	John Gosden	won Yarmouth Class 4 (5f) (0)
15	212	Washington DC D, BF	2	9-3	106-2	5-1	Aidan O'Brien (IRE)	2nd Curragh Listed (5f) (0)
14	13	Hootenanny BF	2	9-3	95-13	7-2f	Wesley Ward (USA)	3rd Pimlico Listed (5f) (0)
13	14	Extortionist D	2	9-3	98-10	16-1	Olly Stevens	won Nottingham Class 5 mdn (5f) (1)
12	321	Hototo D	2	9-3	100-8	14-1	Kevin Ryan	won Ayr Class 4 mdn (5f) (0)
11	221	Frederick Engels D	2	9-3	114T	9-4f	David Brown	won Musselburgh Class 2 (5f) (0)
10	1	Marine Commando D	2	9-3	105-6	9-2	Richard Fahey	won Carlisle Class 5 auct mdn (5f) (0)
09	1	Strike The Tiger D	2	9-3	-	33-1	Wesley Ward (USA)	won Churchill Downs mdn (4½f) (0)

FAVOURITES -£2.25 **TRAINERS IN THIS RACE** (w-pl-r) Wesley Ward 2-0-10, Aidan O'Brien 1-2-10, Richard Fahey 1-2-9, Charlie Appleby 1-1-3, David Evans 0-0-6, David O'Meara 0-1-5, George Margarson 0-0-2, Stan Moore 0-0-7, Richard Hannon 0-0-9, Roger Varian 0-0-4, Tom Dascombe 0-0-7, Bryan Smart 0-0-2

FATE OF FAVOURITES 0010313000 **POSITION OF WINNER IN MARKET** 0217912077

Moorcroft
Racehorse Welfare Centre

PROVIDING THE
VERY BEST OF CARE
FOR OUR WONDERFUL HORSES AWAITING A NEW HOME AND A NEW LIFE

This centre in the south of England was set up to ensure that retired racehorses whatever age, can be re-trained to find another career in life. Much care and attention is given to each individual horse and when fully retrained new homes are found. The centre retains ownership for life and visits these horses every year to ensure that all is well.

This charity depends on generous donations from horse lovers. Many horses need a time for rehabilitation due to injury etc and start to enjoy an easier life after their racing careers. Visits by appointment are welcomed. Please ring Mary Frances, Manager, on 07929 666408 for more information or to arrange a visit.

Huntingrove Stud, Slinfold, West Sussex RH13 0RB
Tel: 07929 666408 | moorcroftracehorse@gmail.com | www.moorcroftracehorse.org.uk

FIVE OF THE BEST . . .

COURSE FORM IS OFTEN KEY

Since Ascot reopened its doors in 2006 following redevelopment there has been a perception that horses either love the track or loathe it. Of last year's 30 Royal Ascot winners, 11 boasted winning or placed form at the track (37 per cent) – and remember the two-year-olds would have had little opportunity to go there. Those with strong course form included 33-1 Queen Anne Stakes stunner Accidental Agent and Godolphin sprint king Blue Point, who had posted two victories there in 2017.

EXPERIENCE ON SAND USEFUL

Another perception is that good to firm ground at Ascot suits horses who act well on an all-weather surface – excluding Southwell's Fibresand – and the results from 2018 add weight to this theory. Twelve winners had either won or been placed on the all-weather, including two of the first-day Group 1 winners, Accidental Agent *(right)* and Without Parole. Royal Hunt Cup hero Settle For Bay had been successful four times at Dundalk.

A RECENT RUN IS IMPORTANT

A standout stat from 2018 is that 13 of the 30 races (43 per cent) were won by a horse with two previous runs that year. Seven went to horses with three runs, six winners arrived on the back of just one run and three winners had run four times. Only one horse made a winning seasonal reappearance at Royal Ascot, 33-1 Bacchus *(right)* in the Wokingham Handicap.

DON'T FORGET THE JUMPS TRAINERS

Trainers more renowned for their exploits over jumps have dominated the Ascot Stakes in recent years, particularly Willie Mullins. Only Karen McLintock, who trained runner-up Dubawi Fifty, stood in the way of an incredible Mullins 1-2-3-4 last year – he was responsible for the winner Lagostovegas, third Stratum, fourth Chelkar and fifth Whiskey Sour. David Pipe, Nicky Henderson and Jonjo O'Neill have also trained the winner of this race since 2010.

FEWER SURPRISES ON FAST GROUND

When the ground is good to firm – as it was throughout the 2018 meeting – it is reasonable to assume there will be fewer upsets than if underfoot conditions are soft or heavy. Only two of last year's winners could be described as out-of-the-ordinary shocks – 33-1 Accidental Agent in the Queen Anne and 25-1 Signora Cabello in the Queen Mary. In fact, 23 of the 30 winners (77 per cent) started at odds of 10-1 or lower. The sole odds-on winner was 4-7 Crystal Ocean in the Hardwicke Stakes, testament to the ferocity of the week's competition.

TEMPER BY NEIL RANKIN

The Windsor Enclosure welcomes a celebrity chef for the first time with Neil Rankin, founder of the Temper restaurant in London's West End, serving up a menu of sizzling barbecue feasts including aged cheeseburger tacos, grilled spring chicken and succulent steaks. Takeaway options are also available, such as fish tacos, 'Ginger Pig' burgers and salty chips. *Windsor Enclosure; pre-booking not required*

QUEEN ANNE KITCHEN BY JAMES TANNER

From £19 per person, guests at this walk-up option by TV chef and restaurateur James Tanner *(above)* can enjoy a seated al fresco experience with signature dishes such as steak burger, Brixham crab salad, seared sea bass and lemon posset with English berries. *Queen Anne Enclosure, Queen Anne Lawn; pre-booking not required*

BANDSTAND KITCHEN & BAR

From £14 per person, this seated restaurant serves classic dishes including the Ascot brunch, buttermilk chicken, sirloin steak sandwich, smoked salmon

fishcakes and sage gnocchi, alongside a selection of salads, plus bar snacks and pastries. Conveniently located near the Bandstand with plenty of outdoor seating. *Queen Anne Enclosure, Bandstand Lawn; pre-booking not required*

1768 GRILL & TEA ROOMS

From £30 per person, this relaxed restaurant with a tea-room ambience and seated dining specialises in lobster and steak lunches, along with a brand-new afternoon tea menu designed by Master Patissier Eric Lanlard offering a selection of sandwiches, scones and handmade cakes and strawberry preserve (£38 per person). *Queen Anne Enclosure, Pavilion Lawn; available to pre-book on 0844 346 3000 or walk-up on the day*

WINDSOR GREYS

A selection of cured salmon, lobster, carved sirloin of beef, summer salads and indulgent desserts. Browse this buffet and enjoy a complimentary glass of wine for £72 per head. Alternatively enjoy seafood and meat platters in the Windsor Greys Gardens. Sharing platters from £36. *Royal Enclosure; not available to pre-book, enquire on the day*

DAY THREE

*G*old Cup day – or Ladies' Day to those whose principal interest is the fashion – is one of the highlights of the racing year with a card tailored to suit every taste.

Established in 1807, the Gold Cup is the meeting's oldest race and a traditional bulwark against the increasing dominance of speed in racing and breeding. Whereas Royal Ascot's shortest races last barely a minute, Thursday's Group 1 highlight unfolds over two and a half miles and more than four minutes of racing, often building to a compelling conclusion.

Another part of the Gold Cup's enduring appeal is that many winners become firm favourites by competing again over the next two or three seasons. The expected return of Stradivarius to defend his crown will ensure this year's race is one of the highlights of the week again.

There is a fast start to the day with the Group 2 Norfolk Stakes for two-year-olds. In complete contrast to the Gold Cup, this race tests the raw speed of precocious juveniles over the minimum distance of five furlongs.

The other Group 2 contest on the card is the Ribblesdale Stakes, the meeting's

middle-distance feature for three-year-old fillies. Run over a mile and a half, the race often attracts fillies who have graduated from the Oaks at Epsom or at least one of the trials.

The other three races are also restricted to three-year-olds. There is the Hampton Court Stakes, a Group 3 event that was formerly run as the Churchill Stakes on Ascot Heath day when the royal meeting

comprised four days, while two competitive handicaps round off the day.

Race five is the Britannia Stakes, which is basically the Royal Hunt Cup for three-year-old colts and geldings. A maximum field of 30 is guaranteed and the winner is likely to have half a stone in hand of the handicapper and go on to make his mark in Listed or even Group company.

The distance then moves back up to a mile and a half for the King George V Stakes, which is usually won by a lightly raced improver from a powerful stable.

Thursday June 20

RUNNING ORDER

2.30 **Norfolk Stakes** (Group 2) *Last year's winner: Shang Shang Shang 5-1*	**5f** 2yo	£100,000
3.05 **Hampton Court Stakes** (Group 3) *Last year's winner: Hunting Horn 5-1*	**1m2f** 3yo	£90,000
3.40 **Ribblesdale Stakes** (Group 2) *Last year's winner: Magic Wand 100-30*	**1m4f** 3yo fillies	£200,000
4.20 **Gold Cup** (Group 1) *Last year's winner: Stradivarius 7-4jf*	**2m4f** 4yo+	£500,000
5.00 **Britannia Stakes** (Heritage Handicap) *Last year's winner: Ostilio 10-1*	**1m** 3yo colts and geldings	£120,000
5.35 **King George V Stakes** (Handicap) *Last year's winner: Baghdad 9-1*	**1m4f** 3yo	£90,000

*Race
value
is total
prize-
money*

2.30 Norfolk Stakes

THIS is the meeting's third Group 2 race for two-year-olds, following the Coventry and Queen Mary Stakes, and its distinguishing feature is that it is open to both sexes over the minimum distance of five furlongs.

Possibly because of the race distance, the Norfolk has a mixed record of producing enduring stars. Six of the last ten winners failed to notch another victory that year but three of the other four went on to Group 1 success (and the fourth took the Group 2 Gimcrack).

As this is often the major target for a precocious juvenile, it is no surprise to find that most winners have been pushed hard enough beforehand to achieve an adjusted RPR well into three figures and you have to go all

Key trends
▶ *Lost maiden tag, ten winners in ten runnings*
▶ *By a sire with a stamina index of 6.7f to 8.3f, 10/10*
▶ *Adjusted RPR of at least 103, 8/10*
▶ *Won last time out, 8/10*
▶ *Won over 5f, 6/10*
▶ *Recorded pre-race RPR of at least 88 and a Topspeed figure of at least 74, 6/10 (two exceptions were unrated US winners)*
▶ *Won most recent start by at least two lengths, 6/10*

Other factors
▶ *Five were once-raced winners. The other five were all beaten on their debut*
▶ *Two of the winners yet to win over the trip had won over 4½f and were trained by Wesley Ward*

the way back to 1990 to find the last maiden who scored a first win here.

The extent to which connections know what they have on their hands is clear from the winning odds, with only three of the last 20 winners going off bigger than 10-1.

It is almost essential to come here off the back of a victory, with 18 of the last 20 winners having done so (the two exceptions had been unplaced in Listed races).

Along with the ever-dangerous Aidan O'Brien, trainers known for fast horses have done well, including Wesley Ward, Richard Hannon, William Haggas, Clive Cox, Kevin Ryan and Robert Cowell. Another to note is Mark Johnston, who won in 2003 and has had a second, third and fourth in the last four runnings.

Story of the last ten years

	FORM	WINNER	AGE & WGT	Adj RPR	SP	TRAINER	BEST RPR LAST 12 MONTHS (RUNS SINCE)
18	1	**Shang Shang Shang**	2 8-12	99-15	5-1	Wesley Ward (USA)	won Keeneland (4½f) (0)
17	3216	**Sioux Nation**	2 9-1	103-10	14-1	Aidan O'Brien (IRE)	won Cork mdn (6f) (1)
16	1	**Prince Lir** D	2 9-1	105-11	8-1	Robert Cowell	won Beverley Class 2 (5f) (0)
15	6321	**Waterloo Bridge** D	2 9-1	97-23	12-1	Aidan O'Brien (IRE)	won Tipperary mdn (5f) (0)
14	211	**Baitha Alga**	2 9-1	110-2	8-1	Richard Hannon	won Woodcote Stakes Listed (6f) (0)
13	1	**No Nay Never**	2 9-1	104-10	4-1	Wesley Ward (USA)	won Keeneland (4½f) (0)
12	1	**Reckless Abandon** D	2 9-1	107-6	4-1	Clive Cox	won Doncaster Class 5 mdn auct (5f) (0)
11	1	**Bapak Chinta** D	2 9-1	107-6	6-1	Kevin Ryan	won Hamilton Class 5 mdn (5f) (0)
10	314	**Approve** D	2 9-1	104-7	16-1	William Haggas	4th Woodcote Stakes Listed (6f) (0)
09	21	**Radiohead** D	2 9-1	105-14	10-1	Brian Meehan	won Bath Class 5 mdn (5f) (0)

FAVOURITES -£10.00

TRAINERS IN THIS RACE (w-pl-r): Aidan O'Brien 2-3-8, Clive Cox 1-0-3, Richard Hannon 1-2-6, Wesley Ward 2-0-7, Charlie Hills 0-0-2, Peter Chapple-Hyam 0-1-3, James Given 0-0-4, Karl Burke 0-1-2, Mark Johnston 0-2-10, Richard Fahey 0-0-4, Tom Dascombe 0-0-4

FATE OF FAVOURITES 5606253520 **POSITION OF WINNER IN MARKET** 4632233593

Injured Jockeys Fund

We provide appropriate support in a prompt and sympathetic manner to those jockeys, past or present, who are injured, unable to ride, or generally in need.

As a not-for-profit, self funding organisation we are reliant on the support and generosity of our supporters.

To find out how you can become involved and support the Injured Jockeys Fund or make a donation please visit us at:

www.ijf.org.uk or call: 01638 662246

ompassion • Care • Support

Brough Scott MBE
Chairman - Injured Jockeys Fund

THIS Group 3 race for three-year-olds, which was added to the programme when Royal Ascot was extended to five days in 2002 and upgraded to its current level in 2011, can showcase an up-and-coming star, with three of the last five winners going on to Group 1 success (Hawkbill did so on his very next start in the Eclipse in 2016) and another of that quintet, Time Test, also developing into a Group 1 performer as well as a Group 2 winner.

The roll of honour is dominated by the big yards that house plenty of later-developing three-year-olds, with six of the last ten winners having come from Newmarket. Aidan O'Brien won last year with Hunting

Key trends

- ▶ Yet to win at this level or higher, 10/10
- ▶ Adjusted RPR of at least 121, 9/10
- ▶ Rated within 4lb of RPR top-rated, 9/10 (five were top-rated)
- ▶ Won that season, 7/10
- ▶ Top-four finish last time out, 6/10
- ▶ Distance winner, 6/10

Other factors

- ▶ Three had won a handicap that season
- ▶ Five had been beaten in Classic trials, including three who finished 632 in the Dante
- ▶ Three of the four to have finished outside the top four last time out were beaten in either the Derby or the Prix du Jockey Club

Horn, which ended a long gap since back-to-back victories in 2004 and 2005, although he had been knocking on the door with the third in 2016 and the second and fourth in 2017.

There are two main routes to this race – either through handicaps (three of the last six winners) or from the Classic trail (Hunting Horn had finished sixth in the Prix du Jockey Club and third in two Derby trials).

Most winners had done enough to take high rank in the betting, with six of the last ten coming from the top two and only one of the ten priced at bigger than 8-1.

A last-time-out success is a good pointer, although failure to win can be excused if that run was in a Classic or another Group 1.

Story of the last ten years

	FORM	WINNER	AGE	& WGT	Adj RPR	SP	TRAINER	BEST RPR LAST 12 MONTHS (RUNS SINCE)
18	-1336	**Hunting Horn** D	3	9-0	124T	5-1	Aidan O'Brien (IRE)	6th Prix du Jockey Club Gp1 (1m2½f) (0)
17	1325	**Benbatl**	3	9-0	128T	9-2	Saeed Bin Suroor	5th Derby Gp1 (1m4f) (0)
16	111-1	**Hawkbill** D	3	9-0	121-4	11-2	Charlie Appleby	won Newmarket Listed (1m2f) (0)
15	212-1	**Time Test** D	3	9-0	123T	15-8f	Roger Charlton	won Newbury Class 2 hcap (1m2f) (0)
14	2-11	**Cannock Chase** D	3	9-0	122-1	7-4f	Sir Michael Stoute	won Newbury Class 2 hcap (1m2f) (0)
13	311	**Remote** D	3	9-0	127T	9-4f	John Gosden	won Doncaster Class 2 hcap (1m) (0
12	45-24	**Energizer**	3	9-0	122T	15-2	Jens Hirschberger (GER)	4th Cologne Gp2 (1m) (0)
11	28-39	**Pisco Sour**	3	9-0	121-2	20-1	Hughie Morrison	3rd Dante Stakes Gp2 (1m2½f) (1)
10	211	**Afsare** D	3	9-5	117-12	9-4f	Luca Cumani	won Doncaster Class 2 (1m2f) (0)
09	71-56	**Glass Harmonium**	3	9-2	123-4	8-1	Sir Michael Stoute	6th Dante Stakes Gp2 (1m2½f) (0)

FAVOURITES £2.13 **TRAINERS IN THIS RACE** (w-pl-r) Sir Michael Stoute 2-2-9, Charlie Appleby 1-0-4, Saeed Bin Suroor 1-1-9, Aidan O'Brien 1-2-9, Andrew Balding 0-0-3, Richard Hannon 0-1-3

FATE OF FAVOURITES 5100111226 **POSITION OF WINNER IN MARKET** 4106111422

Fighting out the finish of last year's Hampton Court

THIS is the meeting's premier race for middle-distance filles from the Classic generation and often draws runners who have competed in the Oaks or at least the trials.

Five of the last ten winners had run in a Guineas or the Oaks (two), although none finished closer than fourth and that explains why they were going for this Group 2 rather than a top-level target.

To a large extent this race draws still-developing fillies, with seven of the last ten winners having run no more than four times before this assignment (two of the exceptions came from Irish stables), but most of them had shown enough ability to be tried in Pattern company. The top level might be beyond them at this stage but if you remove Group 1

Key trends
▶ *Raced no more than three times at two, 9/10*
▶ *Adjusted RPR of at least 113, 9/10*
▶ *Contested a Listed or Group race, 9/10 (six had won a Group race)*
▶ *Won one of last two starts, 8/10*
▶ *Won over at least 1m2f, 7/10*

Other factors
▶ *Two winners were RPR top-rated, but five of the other eight were between 7lb and 16lb off top*
▶ *Three winners failed to shed their maiden tag the previous season, while two did not run as juveniles*
▶ *Six winners won or made the frame in a Classic trial*

runs that season from the records of the last eight winners, they would show 12 wins, a second and three thirds from 17 runs. That

clearly points towards a high-performing filly who is just short of Group 1 standard.

In the past 13 runnings the winner has come from Newmarket (seven) or Irish stables (six) and in particular Aidan O'Brien has begun to exert his influence with three of the last five winners (he also had the runner-up in 2013).

Stables renowned for middle-distance Classic winners – and often backed by owner-breeders – have dominated, with Saeed Bin Suroor (for Godolphin), John Gosden, Jim Bolger and Dermot Weld on the roll of honour in the past decade.

There have been some big-priced shocks over the years but none of the last 12 winners was outside the top five in the betting, with seven of them in the top two.

Story of the last ten years

FORM	WINNER	AGE & WGT	Adj RPR	SP	TRAINER	BEST RPR LAST 12 MONTHS (RUNS SINCE)
18 7-314	**Magic Wand**	3 9-0	120-5	10-3	Aidan O'Brien (IRE)	won Cheshire Oaks Gp3 (1m3½f) (1)
17 11-35	**Coronet**	3 9-0	114-9	9-1	John Gosden	3rd Prix Saint-Alary Gp1 (1m2f) (1)
16 31-3	**Even Song**	3 9-0	113-16	15-8f	Aidan O'Brien (IRE)	3rd Newmarket Listed (1m2f) (0)
15 8-111	**Curvy**	3 9-0	122-5	9-2	David Wachman (IRE)	won Curragh Gp3 (1m2f) (0)
14 81-10	**Bracelet**	3 9-0	119-7	10-1	Aidan O'Brien (IRE)	won Leopardstown Gp3 (7f) (1)
13 21	**Riposte** D	3 8-12	111-14	9-2	Lady Cecil	2nd Sandown Class 4 mdn (1m2f) (1)
12 8-11	**Princess Highway**	3 8-12	117-14	17-2	Dermot Weld (IRE)	won Naas Gp3 (1m2f) (0)
11 11151	**Banimpire** D	3 8-12	125T	3-1f	Jim Bolger (IRE)	5th Irish 1,000 Guineas Gp1 (1m) (1)
10 21-03	**Hibaayeb** C	3 8-12	125T	4-1j	Saeed Bin Suroor	won Fillies' Mile Gp1 (1m) (2)
09 11	**Flying Cloud**	3 8-12	120-3	5-1	Saeed Bin Suroor	won Saint-Cloud Gp3 (1m2½f) (1)

FAVOURITES: -£0.63

TRAINERS IN THIS RACE (w-pl-r) Aidan O'Brien 3-1-16, Saeed Bin Suroor 2-0-3, John Gosden 1-5-21, Dermot Weld 1-0-1, Jim Bolger 1-1-2, Mark Johnston 0-0-2, Ralph Beckett 0-0-6, Roger Varian 0-1-5, Sir Michael Stoute 0-4-9, William Haggas 0-0-5

FATE OF FAVOURITES: 4112442122 **POSITION OF WINNER IN MARKET:** 3115252143

HOSTIE HATS

We make bespoke and ready to wear hats, fascinators and fedoras for every occasion

We can make hats in bespoke colours to match your outfits at affordable prices

LYons Hill, Chapel Lane, Toynton all Saints, Lincoln PE23 5AF
7974379654
Lucinda@hostihats.co.uk
www.hostiehats.co.uk

THIS is one of the crown jewels of Royal Ascot and the premier staying race of the British Flat season. Despite the extreme distance of 2m4f, the race often produces an enthralling and thrilling contest – as it did again last year when Stradivarius, Vazirabad and Torcedor were separated by barely a length.

Another attractive element is that the best stayers often return year after year and nine horses have won the race more than once in the 40-odd years since Sagaro, one of the greats, started his hat-trick in 1975.

That feat was eclipsed by the four-in-a-row of Yeats in 2006-2009, a sequence that marked the emergence of Aidan O'Brien as the dominant force of recent years. He has won seven of the last 13 runnings with four different horses and saddled the runner-up in three of the last six editions he didn't win.

This is a race where O'Brien habitually has a single representative and clearly his chosen one has to be taken seriously. His 13 runners since 2006 have returned form figures of 1111217612124 and a level-stake profit of +7.7pt.

There is not a wide choice of targets for stayers and almost every recent winner has come down the Sagaro/Henry II route in Britain or via the Vintage Crop/Saval Beg in Ireland.

Eight of the last 12 winners had won at least one of those races en route and another had been runner-up in the Henry II.

The class factor is important, with 17 of the 19 winners since 2000 having previously struck in a Group 1 or Group 2 (12 had won at the highest level). Only the follow-up winners (Yeats and Royal Rebel) and 2005 winner Westerner had scored at this trip before, but just three (all trained by Aidan O'Brien) had yet to win over at least 2m.

Fancied runners have a good record. Only three of the 19 winners since 2000 were outside the top four in the market and 12 were in the top two.

Roll of honour

Longest-priced winner
25-1 Indian Queen (1991)

Shortest-priced winner
1-5 Ardross (1981)

Most successful trainer
7 wins: **Aidan O'Brien**
Yeats (2006, 2007, 2008, 2009), Fame And Glory (2011), Leading Light (2014), Order Of St George (2016)

Most successful jockey
11 wins: **Lester Piggott**
Zarathustra (1957), Gladness (1958), Pandofell (1961), Twilight Alley (1963), Fighting Charlie (1965), Sagaro (1975, 1976, 1977), Le Moss (1979), Ardross (1981, 1982)

Most successful owner
7 wins: **Coolmore partners**
Yeats (2006, 2007, 2008, 2009), Fame And Glory (2011), Leading Light (2014); Order Of St George (2016)

*All figures since 1946

Frankie Dettori jumps for joy after winning on Stradivarius last year

	FORM	WINNER	AGE & WGT	Adj RPR	SP	TRAINER	BEST RPR LAST 12 MONTHS (RUNS SINCE)
18	133-1	**Stradivarius** C	4 9-1	132^{-5}	7-4j	John Gosden	3rd St Leger Gp1 (1m6½f) (2)
17	30-41	**Big Orange** C	6 9-2	131^{-3}	5-1	Michael Bell	won Princess of Wales's Gp2 (1m4f) (6)
16	111-1	**Order Of St George**	4 9-0	137^{T}	10-11f	Aidan O'Brien (IRE)	won Irish St Leger Gp1 (1m6f) (1)
15	41112	**Trip To Paris** C	4 9-0	121^{-10}	12-1	Ed Dunlop	2nd Henry II Stakes Gp3 (2m) (0)
14	110-1	**Leading Light** C	4 9-0	133^{T}	10-11f	Aidan O'Brien (IRE)	won Vintage Crop Stakes Gp3 (1m6f) (0)
13	133-1	**Estimate** C	4 8-11	126^{-4}	7-2f	Sir Michael Stoute	won Sagaro Stakes Gp3 (2m) (0)
12	133-1	**Colour Vision**	4 9-0	134^{T}	6-1	Saeed Bin Suroor	won Sagaro Stakes Gp3 (2m) (0)
11	15-11	**Fame And Glory**	5 9-2	136^{T}	11-8f	Aidan O'Brien (IRE)	5th Prix de l'Arc de Triomphe Gp1 (1m4f) (2)
10	11-	**Rite Of Passage**	6 9-2	119^{-17}	20-1	Dermot Weld (IRE)	won Leopardstown hcap (2m) (0)
09	151-6	**Yeats** CD, BF	8 9-2	138^{T}	6-4f	Aidan O'Brien (IRE)	won Goodwood Cup Gp2 (2m) (3)

WINS-RUNS 4yo 6-7-43, 5yo 1-4-27, 6yo+ 3-9-54 **FAVOURITES** £4.57 **TRAINERS IN THIS RACE** Aidan O'Brien 4-3-10, John Gosden 1-0-7, Saeed Bin Suroor 1-0-9, Sir Michael Stoute 1-1-4, Dermot Weld 1-1-2, Mark Johnston 0-0-2, Andrew Balding 0-0-5

FATE OF FAVOURITES 1510113121 **POSITION OF WINNER IN MARKET** 1914116121

Key trends

▶ Sire stamina index in excess of 9.5f, 10/10
▶ Won within last two starts, 10/10
▶ Adjusted RPR of at least 126, 8/10
▶ Rated within 5lb of RPR top-rated, 8/10 (five were top-rated)

▶ Group-race winner, 8/10 (five had won a Group 1)
▶ Won over at least 2m, 8/10 (both exceptions trained by Aidan O'Brien)

Other factors

▶ Nine winners were competing in the race for the first time
▶ Winners of the Yorkshire Cup finished 0671; Sagaro Stakes 02117273
▶ Six favourites have won in the last decade (including one joint) but Yeats was the only one to have previously scored over the trip

Stradivarius powers home for golden glory 12 months ago

THIS contest over the straight mile is the second of Royal Ascot's three heritage handicaps, sandwiched between the Royal Hunt Cup (Wednesday) and the Wokingham (Saturday), and is open to three-year-old colts and geldings.

Most winners have been lightly raced, with four of the last six having had no more than four outings, and the difficulty of weighing up a host of runners with limited form is reflected in the fact that four winners in the past decade were sent off at 14-1 or bigger and there has been only one winning favourite since 2006.

The only recent winner with a great deal of

Key trends

▶ *Previously contested a handicap, 9/10 (seven had won one)*
▶ *Officially rated between 87 and 96, 9/10*
▶ *At least one top-three finish within last two starts, 9/10*
▶ *Won in current season over 7f or a mile, 9/10*
▶ *Carried no more than 8st 13lb, 8/10*
▶ *Rated within 3lb of RPR top-rated, 8/10 (three top)*

Other factors

▶ *John Gosden hasn't won this for a while, but was successful four times between 1996 and 2001*

Simon Crisford celebrates a first Royal Ascot victory last year

experience was War Envoy (12 runs) for Aidan O'Brien in 2015. He had run in four Group 1 races by then but most winners have been restricted to maiden, novice and latterly handicap company, with every other winner in the past decade having run in a handicap before coming here. Seven of them had won a handicap, five of them last time out.

A good level of form is important, with eight of the last ten winners no more than 3lb off the top on Racing Post Ratings (three of the last seven were top) and the other two only 6lb below.

Getting in on a weight just below 9st might be ideal, with ten of the last 15 winners in the range from 8st 9lb to 8st 13lb.

A tactically astute jockey is a boon. Jamie Spencer has ridden two of the last three winners and four in total, while Ryan Moore also has two recent victories.

Story of the last ten years

	FORM	WINNER		AGE & WGT	OR		SP	TRAINER	BEST RPR LAST 12 MONTHS (RUNS SINCE)
18	2-221	**Ostilio** D		3 8-9	90-3		10-1	Simon Crisford	won Newmarket Class 4 hcap (1m) (0)
17	2135	**Bless Him** D		3 8-9	90-6		25-1	David Simcock	5th Goodwood Class 2 hcap (7f) (0)
16	3-141	**Limitless** D		3 9-1	95T		13-2	Jamie Osborne	won Doncaster Class 4 hcap (1m) (0)
15	-2470	**War Envoy**		3 9-6	104T		10-1	Aidan O'Brien (IRE)	5th Prix Jean-Luc Lagardere Gp1 (7f) (5)
14	312	**Born In China** D		3 8-4	87-1		14-1	Andrew Balding	2nd Newmarket Class 2 hcap (1m) (0)
13	01-41	**Beauty Flame** D		3 8-12	96-6		20-1	Joanna Morgan (IRE)	won Curragh hcap (1m) (0)
12	6-11	**Fast Or Free** D		3 8-10	87T		6-1f	William Haggas	won Newmarket Class 3 hcap (1m) (0)
11	12-21	**Sagramor** D		3 8-13	93-2		8-1	Hughie Morrison	won Haydock Class 2 hcap (1m) (0)
10	71-12	**Ransom Note** D, BF		3 8-10	92-1		9-1	Barry Hills	2nd Newmarket Class 3 hcap (1m) (0)
09	2-315	**Fareer**		3 8-10	92-3		20-1	Ed Dunlop	won Chester Class 2 hcap (7½f) (1)

FAVOURITES -£3.00 **FATE OF FAVOURITES** 0001440600 **POSITION OF WINNER IN MARKET** 0421864305

Like the preceding Britannia, this is a fascinating yet tricky handicap for three-year-olds but this one is over the longer trip of 1m4f and, unlike the Britannia, is open to fillies as well as colts and geldings.

Also in common with the Britannia, this race favours the bigger stables who have the strength in depth that gives them a better chance of housing the right type of lightly raced three-year-old.

Two of the trainers to watch in this and other 1m4f races are Mark Johnston (six winners since 1995) and Sir Michael Stoute (four since 1998). Godolphin trainers have won twice in the past five runnings (Saeed Bin Suroor with Elite Army in 2014 and Charlie Appleby with Space Age the following year).

John Gosden won twice in the 1990s but perhaps

Key trends
▶ *Carried no more than 9st 1lb, 9/10*
▶ *Top-three finish last time, 9/10*
▶ *Officially rated between 85 and 95, 9/10*
▶ *Previously contested a handicap, 9/10 (eight won one)*
▶ *Won earlier in the season, 8/10*
▶ *Drawn in double figures, 8/10*

Other factors
▶ *Only six winners had won between 1m2f and 1m4f. Two of the other four were maidens. Since 1995, Mark Johnston has had six winners and Sir Michael Stoute has had four*

surprisingly he has failed to add to that tally – he went close with runner-up Space Ship in 2013 and last year's third First Eleven and it would not be a surprise if he had a strong challenger again.

Last year's winner Baghdad *(leading, below)* and classy stayer Brown Panther in 2011 are the only recent winners who had raced this far before but one clue to potential stamina can be gleaned from two-year-old form. The last winner who had been unraced at two was Heron Bay in 2007 and nine of the 11 winners since had been tried over 1m-1m2f as juveniles.

Story of the last ten years

	FORM	WINNER	AGE & WGT	OR	SP	TRAINER	BEST RPR LAST 12 MONTHS (RUNS SINCE)
18	41-31	Baghdad D	3 8-12	90-2	9-1	Mark Johnston	won York Class 4 hcap (1m4f) (0)
17	1-12	Atty Persse BF	3 8-7	93-2	7-1	Roger Charlton	2nd Haydock Class 3 hcap (1m2f) (0)
16	21-11	Gold Mount	3 9-3	95-3	13-2	Alan King	won Sandown Class 3 hcap (1m2f) (0)
15	31-51	Space Age	3 8-10	88T	9-1	Charlie Appleby	won Newmarket Class 3 hcap (1m2f) (0)
14	1-31	Elite Army	3 9-1	94-5	4-1j	Saeed Bin Suroor	won Sandown Class 3 hcap (1m2f) (0)
13	4-322	Elidor	3 9-0	88-5	20-1	Mick Channon	2nd Lingfield Listed (1m3½f) (0)
12	12551	Fennell Bay (4ex)	3 8-1	85T	12-1	Mark Johnston	won Sandown Class 2 hcap (1m) (0)
11	1-411	Brown Panther D	3 8-13	91T	4-1j	Tom Dascombe	won Haydock Class 3 hcap (1m4f) (0)
10	2-111	Dandino	3 8-13	91-2	7-1	James Given	won Epsom Class 2 hcap (1m2f) (0)
09	24-09	Cosmic Sun (3oh)	3 7-12	80-6	66-1	Richard Fahey	2nd Ayr Class 2 hcap (1m) (3)

FAVOURITES -£5.00 **FATE OF FAVOURITES:** 4510310000 **POSITION OF WINNER IN MARKET** 0316014325

HORSES TO WATCH

Racing Post experts each give a top tip for the meeting

Tom Segal

THREAT
Coventry Stakes

There hasn't been a more impressive performance by a two-year-old this season than the one put up by Threat when he beat a couple of highly regarded Godolphin rivals at Newmarket. Richard Hannon's juveniles more often than not improve for their debut efforts, so Threat marked himself out as a top-class prospect by clearing right away from an odds-on shot who had shown plenty on his debut. The time was good and Threat will appreciate the step up to 6f. It will take a top-class colt to beat him.

Tom Park

EQUILATERAL
King's Stand Stakes

Charlie Hills's four-year-old has always been held in the highest regard but has been something of a disappointment on the track. However, things have gone much better this season and he produced a devastating turn of foot in the Palace House Stakes before getting collared late on by Mabs Cross. That was a career best and, despite been better off at the weights in that Group 3 than he will be at Royal Ascot, he appears to be improving at a rapid rate of knots. This could be the race where he finally fulfils his rich promise and kickstarts his career at the top level.

Tom Collins

ANNA'S FAST
Queen Mary Stakes

Wesley Ward has a wealth of two-year-old talent again and it's hard to split Anna's Fast and Nayibeth on their first efforts, but he has always been sweet on this daughter of Sawgrass

Handicap winner Fast Anna and the way she blitzed her rivals on her debut at Keeneland in April was impressive. She didn't get the ideal passage that day but seemed to have plenty left at the line, suggesting 5f at Ascot won't be a problem.

Keith Melrose

CROSS COUNTER
Gold Cup

The introduction of the Stayers' Million, won by Stradivarius in its first year, has had the desired effect of increasing quality in the division and Cross Counter looks a particularly formidable challenger. He was an unusually emphatic winner of the Melbourne Cup and dotted up in a Dubai Group 2 in March. He, rather than Stradivarius, could be the biggest catch for the enriched staying programme and it is advised to get involved at around

Threat: impressive on Newmarket debut

5-1, as it may be the last time such a price is available about him for a while.

Paul Kealy

SANDS OF MALI
Diamond Jubilee Stakes

Ascot has seen its fair share of straight-track specialists and Sands Of Mali gives the impression he is just that. He was an excellent second to Eqtidaar in last year's Commonwealth Cup and, although he lost his form afterwards, was back on song when a ready winner of the British Champions Sprint in October. The first run came on good to firm and the next on soft, so conditions are not going to hinder him either way and a horse with his course form and only one Royal Ascot entry is too big at around 14-1.

Graeme Rodway

CALYX
Commonwealth Cup

John Gosden's Kingman colt won't be much of a price but he looks banker material for this Group 1 confined to three-year-old sprinters following an impressive victory in the trial over course and distance on his reappearance after a long layoff. An easy winner of the Coventry Stakes last season, again over course and distance, he has the potential to be champion sprinter this year and

Qabala: fast ground would help her in the Coronation Stakes

should be up to landing this en route to even better things.

Gavin Beech

VENTURA REBEL
Coventry Stakes

Ventura Rebel is attractive at 16-1 for the Coventry, having shaped for all the world like he'll improve again for going up to 6f with the way he flew home to deny red-hot favourite Lady Pauline over 5f at Ascot in May. That form has been crabbed in some quarters, largely because the US raider didn't blitz them as the market expected her to, but that looks a dangerous assumption as the close third is highly regarded and

the front three finished a long way clear of a rival who had won his last two starts.

Pietro Innocenzi

QABALA
Coronation Stakes

Although she lost her unbeaten record when third in the 1,000 Guineas, Qabala probably enhanced her reputation at Newmarket as she was forced to make her move towards the far rail, away from the pace horses. There is always a good chance of fast ground at Ascot in the middle of June, which would boost her prospects further, and she should improve again after just three starts.

FIVE BARS

BRIGADIER GERARD BAR

This hidden gem adjacent to the unsaddling enclosure serves a wide selection of Champagnes, wines, spirits, beers and soft drinks. *Queen Anne Enclosure*

BANDSTAND BAR

Be at the heart of the action next to the famous Bandstand at this bar offering a full range from Champagnes to beers. *Queen Anne Enclosure*

BIT & BRIDLE COCKTAIL BAR

Enjoy a range of refreshing creations including the Royal Ascot Blush – a mix of Beefeater pink gin, lemonade and strawberries. *Royal Enclosure, Level 4*

THE GIN TERRACE

Dedicated gin and cocktail bar serving an array of drinks including Monkey Went To Ascot – Monkey 47 gin with tonic and a slice of cucumber. *Queen Anne Enclosure, Concourse, Grandstand Entrance D*

DANCING BRAVE BAR

This bar at the heart of the grandstand offers draught craft ales from Goose Island and Windsor and Eton Breweries. *Queen Anne Enclosure, Grandstand Entrance B*

DAY FOUR

*T*he introduction of the Commonwealth Cup in 2015 alongside the Coronation Stakes has given day four a Group 1 double-header, making it the only day apart from Tuesday to have more than one top-level race on the programme.

The Commonwealth Cup, exclusively for three-year-old sprinters, has proved a resounding success, not only allowing the younger generation of speedsters the time to mature before taking on older opponents but also having no discernible impact on the competitiveness of the existing Group 1 sprints. The six-furlong contest has produced some thrilling finishes in its short history, along with top-notch form that tends to endure throughout the season.

The Coronation Stakes, over a mile for three-year-old fillies, often attracts graduates from the 1,000 Guineas, Irish 1,000 Guineas and Poule d'Essai des Pouliches in a clash that usually sorts out the Classic form.

Last year Alpha Centauri, having won the Irish 1,000 Guineas, stamped her authority on this division with a six-length success before going on to beat older and male rivals in an electrifying campaign.

Classic form is also on show in the King Edward VII Stakes, the only Group 2

on the card. Often called the Ascot Derby, this mile-and-a-half race regularly attracts horses who have participated in the premier Classic at Epsom.

Friday's programme begins with the Group 3 Albany Stakes for two-year-old fillies over six furlongs on a day when three of the six races are restricted to fillies.

The second of those is the Coronation Stakes and then comes the day's big handicap, the Sandringham Stakes, which is for three-year-old fillies over the straight mile.

The top trainers tend to lay one out for this hotly contested event and the

winner often matures into a high-class performer – the 2016 scorer Persuasive being the best recent example as she went on to lower the colours of the brilliant Ribchester in the Group 1 Queen Elizabeth II Stakes the following autumn.

The card is completed by the Duke of Edinburgh Stakes, a handicap for three-year-olds and upwards over a mile and a half.

This can be a rough race and the winner is usually the one who enjoys a trouble-free passage from a good draw as well as having several pounds in hand of the handicapper.

Friday June 21

RUNNING ORDER

2.30 Albany Stakes (Group 3) *Last year's winner: Main Edition 7-1*	**6f** 2yo fillies	£90,000
3.05 King Edward VII Stakes (Group 2) *Last year's winner: Old Persian 9-2*	**1m4f** 3yo colts and geldings	£225,000
3.40 Commonwealth Cup (Group 1) *Last year's winner: Eqtidaar 12-1*	**6f** 3yo	£500,000
4.20 Coronation Stakes (Group 1) *Last year's winner: Alpha Centauri 11-4f*	**1m** 3yo fillies	£500,000
5.00 Sandringham Stakes (Handicap) *Last year's winner: Agrotera 11-2f*	**1m** 3yo fillies	£90,000
5.35 Duke of Edinburgh Stakes (Handicap) *Last year's winner: Dash Of Spice 7-2f*	**1m4f** 3yo+	£90,000

Race value is total prize-money

THIS Group 3 6f contest for two-year-old fillies, established in 2002 at Listed level and upgraded in 2005, is invariably won by a sharp, precocious juvenile who lacks the scope to train on and scale the heights at three. Although several

Flying home in last year's Albany Stakes won by Main Edition

winners have gone on to better things in their two-year-old days – Cursory Glance won the Group 1 Moyglare Stud Stakes and Brave Anna took the Group 1 Cheveley Park Stakes – for many the Albany is the highlight of their career.

All of the last ten winners had raced at least once and an adjusted RPR of at least 95 has been essential during that period, indicating a good standard is required.

It has not been a great race for favourites, however. Since

Key trends

▶ *No more than two runs, ten winners in last ten runnings*
▶ *Shed maiden tag, 9/10*
▶ *By a sire with a stamina index of at least 7.4f, 9/10*
▶ *At least 7lb off top-rated, 9/10 (exception was top-rated)*
▶ *Ran in a maiden/novice last time out, 8/10*
▶ *Adjusted Racing Post Rating of at least 98, 8/10*

Other factors

▶ *The two maidens who have won since 2007 were both trained by Mick Channon*

Cuis Ghaire triumphed at 8-11 in 2008, only two market leaders have been successful – Newfangled (7-4) and Illuminate (4-1).

Five of the last ten winners have been returned at odds of 14-1 or bigger and that trend has become more pronounced lately, with three of the last five scorers sent off at 14-1, 16-1 and 20-1.

Jamie Spencer is the jockey with the best record in the race with four wins – La Chunga (2005), Nijoom Dubai (2007), Samitar (2011) and Kiyoshi (2013).

Story of the last ten years

	FORM	WINNER	AGE & WGT	Adj RPR	SP	TRAINER	BEST RPR LAST 12 MONTHS (RUNS SINCE)
18	11	**Main Edition** D	2 9-0	104-7	7-1	Mark Johnston	won Goodwood Class 5 nov (6f) (0)
17	11	**Different League** D	2 9-0	96-18	20-1	Matthieu Palussiere (FR)	won Angers conditions stakes (6f) (0)
16	81	**Brave Anna** D	2 9-0	103-14	16-1	Aidan O'Brien (IRE)	won Curragh mdn (6f (0)
15	1	**Illuminate** D	2 9-0	98-12	4-1f	Richard Hannon	won Salisbury Class 3 (5f) (0)
14	1	**Cursory Glance** D	2 9-0	98-10	14-1	Roger Varian	won Kempton Class 5 mdn (6f) (0)
13	41	**Kiyoshi** D	2 8-12	106-15	8-1	Charlie Hills	won Goodwood Class 5 mdn (6f) (0)
12	1	**Newfangled** D	2 8-12	111T	7-4f	John Gosden	won Newmarket Class 4 mdn (6f) (0)
11	3	**Samitar**	2 8-12	95-22	16-1	Mick Channon	3rd Newmarket Class 4 mdn (6f) (0)
10	1	**Memory** D	2 8-12	107-9	15-2	Richard Hannon snr	won Goodwood Class 5 mdn (6f) (0)
09	31	**Habaayib**	2 8-12	102-16	16-1	Ed Dunlop	won Nottingham Class 5 mdn auct (5f) (0)

FAVOURITES -£2.25

TRAINERS IN THIS RACE (w-pl-r) Aidan O'Brien 1-2-11, Ed Dunlop 1-0-3, Richard Hannon 1-0-5, Mark Johnston 1-0-9, Roger Varian 1-0-3, David Evans 0-1-1, James Given 0-0-2, Jeremy Noseda 0-2-5, Keith Dalgleish 0-0-2, Wesley Ward 0-1-8, William Haggas 0-0-3

FATE OF FAVOURITES 2401231520 **POSITION OF WINNER IN MARKET** 5481371793

ELLIOTT

BRITISH SCULPTOR
CHARLES ELLIOTT

"At Full Stretch" 2019 Sculpture

Charles Elliott – Elliott of London

www.elliottoflondon.co.uk

Studio: 01494 758 896

Email: info@elliottoflondon.co.uk

BRITISH  HANDCRAFTED SCULPTURES

THIS Group 2 over 1m4f for three-year-olds comes just under three weeks after the Derby at Epsom and was once officially called the Ascot Derby, as it still is colloquially, such is the close link between the races.

Even though there is only a short time between Epsom and Royal Ascot, many King Edward VII winners have graduated from the Derby, including two of the last three, Across The Stars and Permian, who both finished tenth on the Downs.

Favourites have a poor recent record – only Nathaniel at 11-4 in 2011 has justified market leadership in the last 12 runnings – and winners can come from recognised Classic trials or handicaps (Hillstar in 2013 and Eagle

Key trends

▶ *Adjusted RPR of at least 120, 8/10*

▶ *Yet to win over 1m4f, 8/10*

▶ *Within 7lb of RPR top-rated, 7/10*

▶ *Won earlier in the season between 1m1f and 1m3f, 6/10*

▶ *Ran in a recognised Derby trial, 6/10 (two won)*

Other factors

▶ *No winner had run in Group company at two*

▶ *One winner had landed the Dante, while seven had finished first or second at Newmarket that season*

Top in 2014 were both having their first start in Pattern company).

Sir Michael Stoute, who sent out his first King Edward VII winner in 1983

with Shareef Dancer, must always be respected, having won the race seven times. Along with two winners, he has had a second, third and fourth in the nine runnings since 2010.

Mark Johnston and John Gosden have had three winners apiece. Gosden's best winner was Nathaniel, who went on to great success at Group 1 level, with victories in the King George VI and Queen Elizabeth Stakes and Eclipse Stakes. Since Nathaniel's win in 2011, Gosden has had eight runners with one win, two seconds and a third.

Frankie Dettori has ridden four winners – most recently the Stoute-trained Across The Stars in 2016 – and so has William Buick, who had his fourth success in the last eight runnings with Old Persian last year.

	FORM	WINNER	AGE	& WGT	Adj RPR	SP	TRAINER	BEST RPR LAST 12 MONTHS (RUNS SINCE)
18	7-121	**Old Persian**	3	9-0	120-4	9-2	Charlie Appleby	won Newmarket Stakes Listed (1m2f) (0)
17	32110	**Permian**	3	9-0	128T	6-1	Mark Johnston	won Dante Stakes Gp2 (1m2½f) (1)
16	2-130	**Across The Stars** D	3	9-0	120-2	7-1	Sir Michael Stoute	3rd Lingfield Derby Trial Listed (1m3½f) (1)
15	1-2	**Balios**	3	9-0	123-5	3-1	David Simcock	2nd Newmarket Stakes Listed (1m2f) (0)
14	14	**Eagle Top** BF	3	9-0	114-10	12-1	John Gosden	4th Leicester Class 3 hcap (1m4f) (0)
13	41-22	**Hillstar** BF	3	8-12	118-13	15-2	Sir Michael Stoute	2nd Newbury Class 2 hcap (1m2f) (0)
12	01-51	**Thomas Chippendale**	3	8-12	122-13	9-2	Sir Henry Cecil	won Newmarket Class 3 hcap (1m2f) (0)
11	22-12	**Nathaniel** D, BF	3	8-12	127T	11-4f	John Gosden	2nd Chester Vase Gp3 (1m4½f) (0)
10	11121	**Monterosso**	3	8-12	126-7	7-2	Mark Johnston	won Newmarket Class 2 hcap (1m2f) (0)
09	1-332	**Father Time** BF	3	8-12	123-5	9-1	Sir Henry Cecil	2nd Fairway Stakes Listed (1m2f) (0)

FAVOURITES -£6.25

TRAINERS IN THIS RACE (w-pl-r) John Gosden 2-4-12, Mark Johnston 2-0-4, Sir Michael Stoute 2-2-7, Charlie Appleby 1-0-3, Aidan O'Brien 0-7-15, Andrew Balding 0-1-2, Saeed Bin Suroor 0-0-2, Ralph Beckett 0-0-3, William Haggas 0-0-3

FATE OF FAVOURITES 641422P235 **POSITION OF WINNER IN MARKET** 6213362423

At **Ascot Top Hats Ltd**, we provide new felt Toppers and Vintage Silk Top Hats, as well as refurbishment and fitting services to reshape hats to heads to make them comfortable.

Ascot Top Hats Ltd

By appointment at our workshop please call:
01344 638 838 www.ascot-tophats.co.uk

Unit 24 Space Business Centre,
Molly Millars Lane, Wokingham,
Berks RG41 2PQ

Ascot Top Hats Ltd is a company registered in England and Wales Incorporation Number: 5740259
Registered Office: Beechey House, 87 Church Street, Crowthorne, Berkshire, RG45 7AW

DAY FOUR

THIS Group 1 sprint for three-year-olds was introduced in 2015 with the aim of allowing them to compete at the top level against their contemporaries without having to take on older horses at such an early stage of the season. At the same time the Diamond Jubilee Stakes, another Group 1 Royal Ascot sprint, was closed to three-year-olds.

The new race has proved a huge success, attracting top-class fields in its four runnings and offering a high-level stepping stone to races such as the July Cup and Nunthorpe Stakes where the older horses lie in wait.

Favourites have done well, with two of the four winners (Quiet Reflection and Caravaggio) sent off market leader, and last year provided the biggest surprise to date when Eqtidaar scored at 12-1.

His only success in four previous runs had come in a juvenile maiden on his debut, whereas the first three

winners had plenty of proven form in Group company – in one or more two-year-old races over 5f and 6f, or in that year's early sprints.

Inaugural winner Muhaarar had landed the

Group 2 Gimcrack Stakes at York during his two-year-old career before taking the Group 3 Greenham Stakes on his reappearance at three (recording a then career-best RPR of 119).

The story so far

	FORM	WINNER	AGE	& WGT	Adj RPR	SP	TRAINER	BEST RPR LAST 12 MONTHS (RUNS SINCE)
18	14-24	**Eqtidaar** D	3	9-3	118-9	12-1	Sir Michael Stoute	2nd Ascot Gp3 (6f) (1)
17	111-1	**Caravaggio** CD	3	9-3	131T	5-6f	Aidan O'Brien (IRE)	won Naas Gp3 (6f) (0)
16	11-11	**Quiet Reflection** D	3	9-0	130T	7-4f	Karl Burke	won Haydock Gp2 (6f) (0)
15	13-18	**Muhaarar** D	3	9-3	128-3	10-1	Charlie Hills	won Greenham Stakes Gp3 (7f) (1)

FAVOURITES £0.58

TRAINERS IN THIS RACE (w-pl-r) Aidan O'Brien 1-1-7, Karl Burke 1-0-2, Charlie Hills 1-0-3, Clive Cox 0-1-4, Henry Candy 0-1-2, John Gosden 0-1-2, Wesley Ward 0-0-2, Richard Hannon 0-0-5

FATE OF FAVOURITES 0110 **POSITION OF WINNER IN MARKET** 6115

A delighted Sir Michael Stoute after the victory of Eqtidaar (blue and white striped cap, above) in last year's Commonwealth Cup

Quiet Reflection, the 2016 winner, had won the Group 3 Cornwallis Stakes at Ascot as a juvenile and the Group 2 Sandy Lane Stakes at Haydock (RPR 116) three weeks before Royal Ascot, while Caravaggio went into his hugely trumpeted clash with Harry Angel and Blue Point in 2017 unbeaten in five starts.

Four of those came in Caravaggio's juvenile career, including Royal Ascot's Group 2 Coventry Stakes and the Group 1 Phoenix Stakes at the Curragh, and

he started his three-year-old season with a Group 3 success at Naas (RPR 121).

As a result of their achievements before Royal Ascot, Quiet Reflection and Caravaggio were both top-rated on RPR, while Muhaarar was only 3lb off the top. Eqtidaar, by

contrast, had reached only 107 on RPR before improving to 115 at the royal meeting.

This race is notable as the only Group 1 in Britain for three-year-olds that allows geldings to compete, although no gelding has been successful in the first four runnings.

THIS is the premier race for three-year-old fillies at Royal Ascot and last year featured one of the standout performances of the meeting when Alpha Centauri *(left)* scorched home by six lengths in track-record time.

She was the second consecutive Irish 1,000 Guineas winner to add this race to her roll of honour – following the 2017 success of Winter, who had also won the 1,000 Guineas at Newmarket – and had the winners of the British and French equivalents behind her.

It is a regular occurrence for the Guineas participants from Britain, Ireland and France to go head to head in this contest, which has held Group 1 status since 1988. All but one of the 19 winners since 2000 had run in a Guineas, with eight having

Story of the last ten years

	FORM	WINNER	AGE & WGT	Adj RPR	SP	TRAINER	BEST RPR LAST 12 MONTHS (RUNS SINCE)
18	25-01	**Alpha Centauri** D	3 9-0	128^{-1}	11-4f	Jessica Harrington (IRE)	won Irish 1,000 Guineas Gp1 (1m) (0)
17	1-211	**Winter** D	3 9-0	133^{T}	4-9f	Aidan O'Brien (IRE)	won Irish 1,000 Guineas Gp1 (1m) (0)
16	13-13	**Qemah** D, BF	3 9-0	127^{-4}	6-1	Jean-Claude Rouget (FR)	won Chantilly Gp3 (1m) (1)
15	32-11	**Ervedya** D	3 9-0	129^{-1}	3-1	Jean-Claude Rouget (FR)	won Maisons-Laffitte Gp3 (7f) (1)
14	312-7	**Rizeena** C	3 9-0	127^{T}	11-2	Clive Brittain	won Moyglare Stud Stakes Gp1 (7f) (2)
13	18-21	**Sky Lantern** D	3 9-0	127^{T}	9-2j	Richard Hannon snr	won 1,000 Guineas Gp1 (1m) (0)
12	25-16	**Fallen For You** D, BF	3 9-0	125^{-7}	12-1	John Gosden	2nd May Hill Stakes Gp2 (1m) (3)
11	2-401	**Immortal Verse** D	3 9-0	123^{-5}	8-1	Robert Collet (FR)	won Chantilly Gp2 (1m) (0)
10	318-5	**Lillie Langtry** D	3 9-0	123^{-4}	7-2f	Aidan O'Brien (IRE)	5th Irish 1,000 Guineas Gp1 (1m) (0)
09	31-1	**Ghanaati** D	3 9-0	131^{T}	2-1f	Barry Hills	won 1,000 Guineas Gp1 (1m) (0)

FAVOURITES £5.44

TRAINERS IN THIS RACE (w-pl-r) Aidan O'Brien 2-3-13, Jean-Claude Rouget 2-1-4, John Gosden 1-2-9, Sir Michael Stoute 0-1-5

FATE OF FAVOURITES 1150102611 **POSITION OF WINNER IN MARKET** 1146132411

4.20 Coronation Stakes

been successful in at least one of those Classics and four more placed (the one who hadn't competed in a Guineas was Fallen For You in 2012).

Many winners also achieved a high level of form as juveniles. With any runner who hasn't won a Guineas, the next best indicator is a Group 1 placing at two – 16 of the last 19 winners fell into one of those two categories. Eleven of the 19 were either a Guineas winner or a Group 1 winner at two, though only 2013 winner Sky Lantern was both.

Sir Michael Stoute, who landed his first Coronation with the brilliant Sonic Lady in 1986, has won four times, while Winter's trainer Aidan O'Brien has been successful on three occasions.

Ryan Moore is the most successful jockey in the race's recent history. He has steered home two of the last five winners, Rizeena (2014) and Winter.

There has been a growing trend in recent years for winners of the race to be trained outside Britain. Seven of the last 11 come into that category, with four Irish winners and three French-based scorers, two of which were prepared by Jean-Claude Rouget.

Both of Rouget's

Key trends
▶ *Adjusted RPR of at least 123, 10/10*
▶ *Rated within 7lb of RPR top-rated, 10/10*
▶ *Ran in a European 1,000 Guineas, 9/10*
▶ *Won earlier in the season, 8/10*

Other factors
▶ *Four winners had run in the 1,000 Guineas, where they finished 1171; three ran in France (013) and three in Ireland (511)*
▶ *Winners of the Irish 1,000 Guineas finished 738341611*
▶ *Only four winners had won a Group race as a juvenile*

Roll of honour
Longest-priced winner
25-1 Rebecca Sharp (1997)
Shortest-priced winner
1-6 Humble Duty (1970)
Most successful trainer
5 wins: **Sir Henry Cecil**

Roussalka (1975), One In A Million (1979), Chalon (1982), Chimes Of Freedom (1990), Kissing Cousin (1994)

Most successful jockeys
4 wins: **Joe Mercer**
Festoon (1954), Rosalba (1959), Haymaking (1966), One In A Million (1979)

Lester Piggott
Aiming High (1961), Lisadell (1974), Roussalka (1975), Chalon (1982)

Walter Swinburn
Sonic Lady (1986), Milligram (1987), Marling (1992), Exclusive (1998)

Most successful owners
3 wins: **Sheikh Mohammed**
Sonic Lady (1986), Golden Opinion (1989), Kissing Cousin (1994)

Cheveley Park Stud
Exclusive (1998), Russian Rhythm (2003), Nannina (2006)

Coolmore partners
Sophisticat (2002), Lillie Langtry (2010), Winter (2017)

Niarchos family
Magic Of Life (1988), Chimes Of Freedom (1990), Alpha Centauri (2018)

*All figures since 1946

fillies had contested the Group 1 Poule d'Essai des Pouliches (the French 1,000 Guineas) on their previous start – Ervedya won and Qemah finished third.

This is not the only time in the race's history when overseas raiders have been to the fore. From 1989 to 1996 the race was won by French

stables on three occasions (Andre Fabre, Criquette Head and Elie Lellouche) and two Irish yards (Michael Kauntze and John Oxx).

Fallen For You, who bucks the trends in more ways than one, is the only winner since 2000 who wasn't in the first four in the betting and the only one sent off bigger than 8-1. Ten of the 19 winners in that period were favourite or joint-favourite.

Trainer Jessica Harrington after the success of Alpha Centauri in last year's Coronation Stakes

THE Sandringham, which was introduced to the Royal Ascot programme in 2002 and is now effectively a fillies' Britannia, is a straight-mile handicap restricted to three-year-old fillies and is almost always won by a progressive type. Eleven of the 17 winners had already tasted success that season (seven were last-time-out winners) and Muteela (2014) and Persuasive (2016) both went to Royal Ascot unbeaten in three starts, which included success on the all-weather.

A mark of the developing

Key trends
► *Lost maiden tag, 10/10*
► *Carried no more than 9st 2lb, 7/10*
► *Officially rated between 91 and 104, 7/10*
► *Won over 7f or 1m earlier that season, 7/10*
► *No more than three juvenile starts, 7/10*

Other factors
► *Four winners ran in handicaps as three-year-olds (all four won at least one)*
► *Five winners had contested a Listed or Group race as a three-year-old*

talent that often comes to the fore here is that Persuasive, who won the Sandringham off an official mark of 95, signed off her career the following year by landing the Group 1 Queen Elizabeth II Stakes. Another subsequent Group 1 scorer was 2006 winner Red Evie, who went on to win the Matron Stakes and Lockinge Stakes.

Nine of the 17 winners came from the top two in the betting, including six who had at least a share of favouritism, and only three winners have been bigger than 11-1 (just one of those in the last 11 runnings).

Story of the last ten years

	FORM	WINNER	AGE & WGT	OR	SP	TRAINER	BEST RPR LAST 12 MONTHS (RUNS SINCE)
18	6-21	**Agrotera** D	3 8-7	88-5	11-2f	Ed Walker	2nd Ascot Class 3 cond (1m) (1)
17	142-4	**Con Te Partiro**	3 9-5	102-12	20-1	Wesley Ward (USA)	4th Belmont Park Listed (7f) (0)
16	1-11	**Persuasive**	3 8-9	95T	11-4f	John Gosden	won Chelmsford Class 2 hcp (1m) (0)
15	13-17	**Osaila** CD	3 9-7	107-3	13-2	Richard Hannon	5th Moyglare Stud Stakes Gp1 (7f) (4)
14	1-11	**Muteela**	3 8-13	95T	9-2f	Mark Johnston	won Newmarket Class 3 hcap (1m) (0)
13	41-61	**Annecdote** (1oh)	3 8-7	91T	11-1	Jonathan Portman	won Newbury Class 4 hcap (7f) (0)
12	6-14	**Duntle**	3 9-2	104T	4-1f	David Wachman (IRE)	4th Leopardstown Gp3 (1m) (0)
11	0-512	**Rhythm Of Light**	3 8-12	94T	8-1	Tom Dascombe	2nd Haydock Class 3 hcap (7f) (0)
10	1-428	**Timepiece** CD	3 9-5	105-4	5-1	Sir Henry Cecil	2nd Lingfield Listed (1m3½f) (1)
09	4-531	**Moneycantbuymelove**	3 8-11	96T	9-2f	Michael Bell	won Goodwood Listed (1m2f) (0)

FAVOURITES £16.25 **FATE OF FAVOURITES** 1321012101 **POSITION OF WINNER IN MARKET** 1251512191

Agrotera crosses the line to give Jamie Spencer a fourth Sandringham win

THIS prestigious and valuable 1m4f handicap for three-year-olds and upwards dates back to 1914 and was formerly known as the Bessborough Handicap before being renamed in 1999.

Four-year-olds have the best recent record, with ten of the last 14 winners, including Dash Of Spice last year. He was the fourth successful favourite (outright or joint) in the last seven runnings after a long gap back to the Queen's Blueprint in 1999.

Trouble in running in maximum fields on Ascot's round course is a common occurrence and it is no real surprise that the winner has been returned at 10-1 or bigger in nine of the 19 runnings since Blueprint's success

Winners of this race sometimes go on to make a

Key trends
▶ *Aged four or five, 10/10*
▶ *Drawn in double figures, 10/10*
▶ *Officially rated between 91 and 101, 9/10*
▶ *Achieved best RPR in a Class 2 or 3 handicap, 9/10*
▶ *Top-three finish last time, 9/10 (five won)*
▶ *Ran no more than four times that season, 8/10 (both exceptions trained by Mark Johnston)*

Other factors
▶ *Four of the last seven winners started favourite, including one joint-favourite*

splash in Listed and Group company, with Blueprint (1999) and Young Mick (2006) two of the best examples. Blueprint took the Group 2 Jockey Club Stakes the following year, while Young Mick went on to land the Group 3 Cumberland Lodge Stakes.

Sir Michael Stoute has a long and successful history with the race, having had six winners, while Mark Johnston and Hughie Morrison are two other trainers to note. Remarkably, those three have had 12 of the last 21 winners between them.

The 1m4f handicaps at Newmarket's Guineas meeting, York's Dante fixture and the Epsom Derby meeting often provide good guides. Since the last Irish-trained winner (Katiykha in 2000), 13 of the 18 winners had form at one of those meetings and 11 of those had achieved a top-six placing (though only four won).

A good run at Goodwood in mid-May is also worth noting, while three of the last ten winners had been deemed good enough to run at Royal Ascot the previous year (finishing no better than fifth).

Story of the last ten years

	FORM	WINNER	AGE & WGT	OR	SP	TRAINER	BEST RPR LAST 12 MONTHS (RUNS SINCE)
18	1-221	**Dash Of Spice** D	4 9-3	98^T	7-2f	David Elsworth	won Epsom Class 2 hcap (1m4f) (0)
17	171/8-	**Rare Rhythm** D	5 9-2	97^{-4}	20-1	Charlie Appleby	Seasonal debut (0)
16	22-01	**Kinema**	5 9-4	99^{-3}	8-1	Ralph Beckett	won Goodwood Class 2 hcap (1m6f) (0)
15	342-3	**Arab Dawn** BF	4 9-2	96^T	6-1j	Hughie Morrison	3rd Newmarket Class 2 hcap (1m4f) (0)
14	2-111	**Arab Spring** D	4 9-10	104^{-3}	11-4f	Sir Michael Stoute	won York Class 2 hcap (1m4f) (0)
13	010-3	**Opinion**	4 9-0	95^T	8-1	Sir Michael Stoute	3rd Newmarket Class 2 hcap (1m4f) (0)
12	-1061	**Camborne** D	4 9-4	97^{-1}	11-2f	John Gosden	won Doncaster Class 4 hcap (1m4f) (0)
11	21641	**Fox Hunt** D	4 9-8	99^{-2}	12-1	Mark Johnston	2nd Chester Class 2 hcap (1m2½f) (6)
10	67-42	**Cill Rialaig** C	5 8-11	91^{-3}	16-1	Hughie Morrison	2nd Epsom Class 2 hcap (1m4f) (0)
09	83332	**Drill Sergeant**	4 9-7	101^{-3}	14-1	Mark Johnston	3rd Jockey Club Stakes Gp2 (1m4f) (3)

WINS-PL-RUNS 4yo 7-15-86, 5yo 3-10-49, 6yo+ 0-5-39 **FAVOURITES** £8.25

FATE OF FAVOURITES 0201211201 **POSITION OF WINNER IN MARKET** 8781511481

ROYAL ASCOT

LOCKINGE HOLDS KEY

The Lockinge is the key pointer for the Queen Anne Stakes and backing all 76 who lined up here after taking part in the Newbury contest since 1999 would have found 11 of the 20 winners (14%, +15.41pt). To improve the strike-rate and level-stake profit, it's best to look at those who finished outside the first three in the Lockinge and whose SP at Ascot was less than 40-1, which gives a return of six winners from 31 runners (19%, +43.33pt). This system would have produced a profit even before Accidental Agent's 33-1 success last year after his Lockinge sixth.

FOLLOW GUINEAS FORM

Guineas form has become increasingly important in the Jersey Stakes and Expert Eye's comfortable success in last year's renewal saw him become the eighth winner in the last ten years to have contested one of the European early-season Classics on their latest start. Since 2009 there have been 38 qualifiers from this system, giving a strike-rate of 21% (+42pt).

Expert Eye wins last year's Jersey Stakes, having run in the 2,000 Guineas on his previous start

Key trends

RULE BRITANNIA

The Britannia Handicap can appear to be one of the toughest puzzles for punters to solve but fancied runners have done well in recent years. By focusing on those whose SP was 10-1 or less and fitted these three criteria – officially rated 87 to 96; carried less than 9st 2lb; top-three finish within last two starts – you would have found five of the last ten winners (16%, +13.5pt) from 31 qualifiers, including last year's 10-1 scorer Ostilio.

SIMPLE SYSTEM

Newmarket form is a common theme among King Edward VII winners, as 15 of the 20 winners since 1999 had previously run on the Rowley Mile. Following a system of backing all fancied runners (SP less than 10-1) with Newmarket form would have found all 15 winners from 54 qualifiers (28%, +32pt). Last year's 9-2 winner Old Persian was another case in point as he had run well in all three starts at Newmarket earlier in the season.

JUMP TO IT

Top Irish jumps trainers Willie Mullins and Gordon Elliott have plundered some decent prizes on the Flat in recent years and seem to target the Queen Alexandra on a regular basis. Mullins' fancied runners (priced less than 5-1) have provided two winners from six qualifiers (33%, +1.5pt) and Elliott has been even more efficient with both of his runners obliging – Commissioned at 12-1 in 2016 and Pallasator at 11-2 last year.

THE ITV TEAM

All 30 races of Royal Ascot will be broadcast live on ITV, totalling approximately 30 hours of live coverage across the week. Here some of the team, led by hosts Ed Chamberlin and Francesca Cumani (below), give their tips on where to be and what to do at the big meeting

ED CHAMBERLIN

"The bandstand at the end of each day. As well as being part of Royal Ascot tradition, it's like a free Last Night at the Proms and as a Southampton fan I usually twist the arm of the bandmaster to play When The Saints Go Marching In!"

FRANCESCA CUMANI

"I love the royal procession as not only does it start the whole

week off, but it starts off every day. The Queen is a symbol of Royal Ascot and she's the very heart of the week. So get a good position just before 2pm every day to see the royal carriages come in."

OLI BELL

"The racing is world class at Royal Ascot and whether it's a Group 1 or a big-field handicap it's competitive with a capital C. For me the race of the week is the Gold Cup for the stayers."

JASON WEAVER

"Where else do you get to see the best of every division – sprinters, stayers and milers of all ages – over perfect turf? Nowhere else on the globe. So scrub up well, buy a new outfit, and bring plenty of money to punt."

RICHARD HOILES

"For all the wonderful pomp and ceremony at Royal Ascot, the horses are the real stars and if you get a good spot around the pre-parade ring, away from the buzz, you'll get to see them up close before they run as well as understand the seriousness of their connections as they prepare them."

LUKE HARVEY

"The horses at Royal Ascot are the best of the best and the elite athletes of our sport. Don't miss seeing them in the parade ring before the races, as even with an untrained eye you'll be able to see for yourself the ones who stand out and who you want to put your money on."

MATT CHAPMAN

"If you're having a bet, I'd recommend looking at the pool betting as the odds hold up well at the big meetings."

FIVE PLACES FOR FOOD ON THE GO

BUBBLES & WRAPS

Choose from a selection of wraps including onion bhaji, southern fried buttermilk chicken and Royal Estate spiced lamb, available to enjoy alongside a glass of prosecco for £14. *Queen Anne Enclosure*

SUSSEX CHARMER CHEESE ON TOAST

This tasty treat by Sussex dairy farmers Bookham & Harrison is always a favourite and their stall has a prime location at the east end of the Bandstand Lawn. *From £6 per person; Queen Anne Enclosure, Grandstand Entrance D*

WOOD FIRED PIZZA COMPANY

Options include the Americano pizza or the Big Feast deal – four pizzas, four soft drinks and dough balls to share. Located on the east end of the grandstand with a great view over the Bandstand for the evening singalong. *From £9 per person; Queen Anne Enclosure, Grandstand Entrance C*

THE BURGER KITCHEN BY JAMES TANNER

Gourmet burgers produced to celebrity chef James Tanner's specification, such as steak burger or mushroom burger. *From £8 per person; Queen Anne Enclosure*

THE JOINT

Choose from BBQ pork buns, chicken wings and deep fried mac 'n' cheese, served with chips. *Windsor Enclosure*

"Much bigger than I expected…much higher quality of art"

F R E S H :

CONTEMPORARY
ART FAIR
ASCOT RACECOURSE
20-22 SEPTEMBER 2019

54 leading UK Galleries: 600 UK & international artists: 5000 original paintings & sculptures

Visit: freshartfair.net

DAY FIVE

Nobody could say Royal Ascot has suffered any dilution in quality since the meeting was expanded to five days in 2002 and the meeting concludes with a stunning final-day programme that is every bit as good as the previous four.

The Group 1 highlight is the Diamond Jubilee Stakes, a six-furlong sprint open to four-year-olds and upwards, which some will remember as the Cork and Orrery Stakes in days of old. This race has a reputation for attracting the best sprinters from all parts of the globe, with winners from Australia – most notably supermare Black Caviar in 2012 – Hong Kong and the United States in recent years.

For the fourth consecutive day the two-year-olds open the card, this time in the seven-furlong Chesham Stakes. The distance of this Listed race attracts the less precocious juveniles who are likely to excel at a mile or further during their three-year-old careers.

Churchill, who went on to land the 2,000 Guineas and Irish 2,000 Guineas in 2017, scored his first career success in this race.

The Group 3 Jersey Stakes has been moved from Wednesday to a more prominent position as the second race on the Saturday card and rightly so given that two of the last three winners, Ribchester (2016) and Expert Eye (2018), went on to be Group 1 milers.

The Group 2 Hardwicke Stakes is a Royal Ascot favourite for many and can be an excellent guide to the outcome of the King George VI and Queen Elizabeth Stakes at the royal track in July.

Punters have adopted the saying "if in doubt back Sir Michael Stoute" in this 1m4f race for four-year-olds and upwards, with the Newmarket trainer having won an incredible 11 times, including last year with Crystal Ocean.

The last big handicap of the week is the Wokingham Stakes over six furlongs. Like the week's other heritage handicaps, the race habitually attracts a big field of up to 30 runners and a competitive betting market.

After that helter-skelter sprint, the action switches to the other extreme with the 2m6f Queen Alexandra Stakes, the much-loved traditional closing event of the meeting. Fittingly, as Royal Ascot is uniquely special in so many aspects, it is the longest Flat race staged in Britain each year.

Saturday June 22

RUNNING ORDER

| 2.30 **Chesham Stakes** (Listed) | **7f** 2yo | £90,000 |
| Last year's winner: Arthur Kitt 13-2 | | |

| 3.05 **Jersey Stakes** (Group 3) | **7f** 3yo | £90,000 |
| Last year's winner: Expert Eye 8-1 | | |

| 3.40 **Hardwicke Stakes** (Group 2) | **1m4f** 4yo+ | £225,000 |
| Last year's winner: Crystal Ocean 4-7f | | |

| 4.20 **Diamond Jubilee Stakes** (Group 1) | **6f** 4yo+ | £600,000 |
| Last year's winner: Merchant Navy 4-1 | | |

| 5.00 **Wokingham Stakes** (Heritage Handicap) | **6f** 3yo+ | £175,000 |
| Last year's winner: Bacchus 33-1 | | |

| 5.35 **Queen Alexandra Stakes** (Conditions) | **2m6f** 4yo+ | £90,000 |
| Last year's winner: Pallasator 11-2 | | |

Race value is total prize-money

THIS Listed contest is now the final race for two-year-olds and at 7f it is the longest of the week for that age group. It is designed to provide an early stamina test for youngsters, being open only to horses whose sires won over a distance of 1m2f-plus in their own racing careers.

It is no surprise, then, that Aidan O'Brien – the dominant force in Classics both at a mile and over middle distances – has won three times in the last eight years, including two of the last three runnings with Churchill and September.

O'Brien first won the race in 1999 with Bach but then did not strike again until 2011 with Maybe. He is always likely to field a strong candidate nowadays and his 11

Key trends

▶ *By a sire with a stamina index of at least 8.7f, nine winners in last ten runnings*
▶ *Recorded Topspeed figure of at least 64, 7/10*
▶ *Raced just once, 8/10 (five had won)*
▶ *Adjusted RPR of at least 91, 8/10*
▶ *Rated within 9lb of RPR top-rated, 7/10*

Other factors

▶ *In 2017, September became the first winner to have previously won over 7f since Bach in 1999 (also trained by Aidan O'Brien)*
▶ *The record of fillies is 2-36*

runners in the past decade have produced three wins, two seconds and a third – interestingly, his three winners have come in years when he fielded just a single representative (from seven runners in total).

The other main trainer to watch is John Gosden, who has had a winner from just five runners in the past decade. Again it may pay to take note when he has only a single runner.

Most of the big-priced winners have come in the past decade but in the longer term, since the distance was raised to 7f in 1996, the majority of winners have been well fancied. Seven of the 23 winners in that period had market leadership, with a further 12 in the top four in the betting.

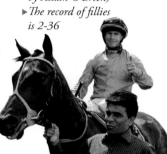

Thumbs up: Richard Kingscote and Arthur Kitt after last year's win

Story of the last ten years

	FORM	WINNER	AGE & WGT	Adj RPR	SP	TRAINER	BEST RPR LAST 12 MONTHS (RUNS SINCE)
18	1	**Arthur Kitt**	2 9-3	100-9	13-2	Tom Dascombe	won Haydock Class 4 nov (6f) (0)
17	1	**September** D	2 8-12	107T	11-8f	Aidan O'Brien (IRE)	won Leopardstown mdn (7f) (0)
16	3	**Churchill** BF	2 9-3	95-9	8-11f	Aidan O'Brien (IRE)	3rd Curragh mdn (6f) (0)
15	1	**Sunny Way**	2 9-3	91-7	14-1	Eoghan O'Neill (FR)	won Maisons-Laffitte mdn (6f) (0)
14	4	**Richard Pankhurst** BF	2 9-3	87-23	10-1	John Gosden	4th Newmarket Class 4 mdn (6f) (0)
13	3	**Berkshire**	2 9-3	90-11	16-1	Paul Cole	3rd Newbury Class 4 mdn (6f) (0)
12	41	**Tha'ir**	2 9-3	109-1	9-2	Saeed Bin Suroor	won Ripon Class 5 mdn (6f) (0)
11	1	**Maybe**	2 8-12	109T	5-2f	Aidan O'Brien (IRE)	won Naas mdn (6f) (0)
10	1	**Zaidan**	2 9-3	98-3	7-1	Clive Brittain	won Doncaster Class 5 mdn (5f) (0)
09	42	**Big Audio**	2 9-3	91-12	22-1	Richard Hannon snr	2nd Doncaster Class 5 mdn (6f) (0)

FAVOURITES £-2.40

TRAINERS IN THIS RACE (w-pl-r) Aidan O'Brien 3-3-11, John Gosden 1-1-5, Paul Cole 1-1-4, Charlie Hills 0-0-2, James Tate 0-0-2, Eve Johnson Houghton 0-0-2, Mark Johnston 0-2-14, Michael Bell 0-0-2, Richard Hannon 0-0-4, Simon Crisford 0-0-2

FATE OF FAVOURITES 2014232110 **POSITION OF WINNER IN MARKET** 0413846113

nirvana
S P A

Escape to the spa...

Spa visits from £47

Wokingham, Berkshire | www.nirvanaspa.co.uk

THE distance of seven furlongs in this Group 3 race makes it something of a battleground between Classic pretenders dropping back from a mile and sprinters trying to stretch out their stamina. Last year Expert Eye was in the first category, having finished tenth in the 2,000 Guineas, although he later proved himself at the longer distance when he ended the season with victory in the Breeders' Cup Mile at Churchill Downs.

Expert Eye continued the recent trend for those who had run in a Guineas to hold sway, with eight of the last ten winners having run in at least one of the mile Group 1s at Newmarket, the Curragh or in France.

That emphasis on having

Key trends

▶ *Adjusted RPR of at least 122, 9/10*
▶ *First or second in one or both of last two starts, 9/10*
▶ *Rated within 6lb of RPR top-rated, 9/10*
▶ *Ran in a Guineas, 8/10*
▶ *Distance winner, 7/10*
▶ *Won as a three-year-old, 6/10*
▶ *Top-three finish last time out, 6/10*

Other factors

▶ *Fillies don't have a great record but won in 2010 and 2012 (Rainfall and Ishvana)*
▶ *Winners of the King Charles II at Newmarket have finished 5237420*
▶ *Six winners had run in Classic trials but only one was successful*

been highly tried is also evident when looking at the two-year-old records of past winners. Given where Ascot falls in the calendar it is no surprise that 18 of the last 20 winners raced at two but perhaps more telling is the fact that, among them, 14 had a first-four finish to their name at Group level during their juvenile season.

That requirement to have performed to a high level is further illustrated by the peak RPRs of winners heading into the race, with 16 of the last 20 winners having previously run to an RPR of 106+.

The last three winners had already reached a considerably higher level, with RPRs of 113 for Ribchester, 118 for Le Brivido and 116 for Expert Eye.

Story of the last ten years

	FORM	WINNER	AGE & WGT	Adj RPR	SP	TRAINER	BEST RPR LAST 12 MONTHS (RUNS SINCE)
18	19-20	**Expert Eye** D	3 9-1	129^T	8-1	Sir Michael Stoute	won Vintage Stakes Gp2 (7f) (3)
17	1-12	**Le Brivido**	3 9-1	131^T	2-1f	Andre Fabre (FR)	2nd Poule d'Essai des Poulains Gp1 (1m) (0)
16	1-2d3	**Ribchester**	3 9-6	122$^{.5}$	7-1	Richard Fahey	won Mill Reef Stakes Gp2 (6f) (2)
15	113-7	**Dutch Connection** D	3 9-4	118$^{.9}$	14-1	Charlie Hills	3rd National Stakes Gp1 (7f) (1)
14	12-13	**Mustajeeb** D	3 9-4	124$^{.4}$	9-2j	Dermot Weld (IRE)	won Amethyst Stakes Gp3 (1m) (1)
13	3-142	**Gale Force Ten** D	3 9-1	128^T	9-2f	Aidan O'Brien (IRE)	2nd Irish 2,000 Guineas Gp1 (1m) (0)
12	29132	**Ishvana** D	3 8-12	125$^{.2}$	20-1	Aidan O'Brien (IRE)	2nd Irish 2,000 Guineas Gp1 (1m) (0)
11	132-6	**Strong Suit** C	3 9-6	122$^{.6}$	11-1	Richard Hannon snr	won Coventry Stakes Gp2 (6f) (3)
10	12	**Rainfall** D	3 8-12	122$^{.5}$	8-1	Mark Johnston	2nd Haydock Listed (6f) (0)
09	19-10	**Ouqba** D	3 9-1	126$^{.2}$	12-1	Barry Hills	won Free Handicap (7f) (1)

FAVOURITES £1.25

TRAINERS IN THIS RACE (w-pl-r) Aidan O'Brien 2-3-13, Sir Michael Stoute 1-2-4, Mark Johnston 1-0-5, Charlie Hills 1-0-7, William Haggas 0-3-9, Andrew Balding 0-0-3, Brian Meehan 0-0-4, David Elsworth 0-0-3, Hugo Palmer 0-0-3, Jeremy Noseda 0-1-6, John Gosden 0-1-12, Marco Botti 0-0-1, Roger Varian 0-1-5, Saeed Bin Suroor 0-2-8

FATE OF FAVOURITES 0623110610 **POSITION OF WINNER IN MARKET** 7558116213

THIS Group 2 race over 1m4f is for four-year-olds and upwards and often provides a showcase for horses who were in the Derby picture the previous year – and sometimes signals the blossoming of a high-class talent who will go on to greater achievements.

The last 11 winners were all four-year-olds and they had followed similar career paths to this point, with nine of them having competed the previous year in at least one of the St Leger, the Great Voltigeur Stakes at York or the King Edward VII Stakes at Royal Ascot.

The Great Voltigeur appears most commonly in their records – three won at York, two were runner-up and two were unplaced. The previous year's result of that contest is always a good place

Key trends

▶ *Aged four, 10/10*
▶ *Group-race winner, 10/10*
▶ *Won over at least 1m4f, 10/10*
▶ *Adjusted RPR of at least 129, 9/10*
▶ *Finished in first three in a Listed or Group race that season, 9/10*

Other factors

▶ *Five favourites have won in the last decade*
▶ *Ormonde Stakes winners have finished 1051755*
▶ *Four of Sir Michael Stoute's last six winners ran at Chester earlier in the season – two in the Huxley (12) and two in the Ormonde (11)*
▶ *Two of Aidan O'Brien's last three winners ran in Epsom's Coronation Cup (36)*

to look for the winner of this race.

Of the five who had run in the previous year's St Leger,

last year's winner Crystal Ocean had finished second and two more had been third, while 2017 scorer Idaho unseated at Doncaster but had previously been third in the Derby and second in the Irish Derby. One of the four who ran in the King Edward VII had won, with Crystal Ocean finishing third and the other two unplaced.

As for current-season form, the Coronation Cup at Epsom, the Gordon Richards Stakes at Sandown (won last year by Crystal Ocean) and middle-distance races at Chester are key staging posts.

The market has been a good guide, with ten of the last 13 winners having come from the first three in the betting. The six successful favourites in that period were trained by Sir Michael Stoute or Aidan O'Brien.

Story of the last ten years

	FORM	WINNER	AGE & WGT	Adj RPR	SP	TRAINER	BEST RPR LAST 12 MONTHS (RUNS SINCE)
18	12-11	**Crystal Ocean** D	4 9-1	135ᵀ	4-7f	Sir Michael Stoute	won Newbury Gp3 (1m4f) (0)
17	1U5-6	**Idaho** D	4 9-1	133⁻¹	9-2	Aidan O'Brien (IRE)	2nd Irish Derby Gp1 (1m4f) (4)
16	53-11	**Dartmouth** CD	4 9-1	129⁻⁷	10-1	Sir Michael Stoute	won Ormonde Stakes Gp3 (1m5½f) (0)
15	237-1	**Snow Sky** D	4 9-1	130⁻⁸	12-1	Sir Michael Stoute	won Yorkshire Cup Gp2 (1m6f) (0)
14	21-22	**Telescope** D	4 9-1	130ᵀ	7-4f	Sir Michael Stoute	2nd Huxley Stakes Gp3 (1m2½f) (0)
13	58-22	**Thomas Chippendale** CD	4 9-0	129⁻⁶	8-1	Lady Cecil	won King Edward VII Stakes Gp2 (1m4f) (4)
12	132-1	**Sea Moon** D	4 9-0	139ᵀ	3-1f	Sir Michael Stoute	won Great Voltigeur Stakes Gp2 (1m4f) (3)
11	/11-1	**Await The Dawn** D	4 9-0	139ᵀ	4-6f	Aidan O'Brien (IRE)	won Huxley Stakes Gp3 (1m2½f) (0)
10	73-11	**Harbinger** D	4 9-0	140ᵀ	8-11f	Sir Michael Stoute	won Ormonde Stakes Gp3 (1m5½f) (0)
09	5-331	**Bronze Cannon** D	4 9-3	127⁻⁵	8-1	John Gosden	won Jockey Club Stakes Gp2 (1m4f) (0)

WINS-RUNS 4yo 10-8-52, 5yo 0-5-17, 6yo+ 0-5-23 **FAVOURITES** £1.72

TRAINERS IN THIS RACE (w-pl-r) Sir Michael Stoute 6-1-16, Aidan O'Brien 2-1-7, John Gosden 1-2-8, Mark Johnston 0-1-2, Ed Dunlop 0-2-5, Roger Varian 0-1-6, Saeed Bin Suroor 0-1-9, William Haggas 0-1-3

FATE OF FAVOURITES 2111S16041 **POSITION OF WINNER IN MARKET** 3111414621

DAY FIVE

THIS is the big 6f sprint of the week for older horses (open only to four-year-olds and upwards since the advent of the Commonwealth Cup for three-year-olds). Connections usually choose between this race and the King's Stand over 5f on the Tuesday but sometimes runners contest both races and Australian raider Choisir completed the double in 2003.

Since the race was upgraded to Group 1 in 2002 there have been 17 winners and eight of them were priced in double figures, with only three successful favourites. However, even most of the longer-priced winners brought a strong level of form, with 13 of the 17 having been placed at least in a Group 1 in the previous 12 months (eight had won), and the other four at least having competed at that level.

Generally the longer-priced winners have come from the group who had been placed in a Group 1 but not yet won at that level. The main races to check for that type of horse are the previous year's running of this race, the July Cup and Haydock Sprint Cup.

The British Champions Sprint, run over course and distance the previous October, is fast developing

into a key guide. Three of the last four British or Irish winners had run there, finishing 121, with the exception being last year's winner Merchant Navy, who was trained by Aidan O'Brien but had been transferred only recently from Australia.

The best prep race has been the Duke of York Stakes, with five of the ten British-trained winners since 2002 having run there for finishing positions of 03255 (O'Brien's Starspangledbanner also prepped there in 2010, finishing fifth).

One explanation for the step up in performance from the Duke of York (and the fact that only five of the last 17 winners had scored on their previous outing) is that the ground often changes from softish in May to much faster in June.

Roll of honour

Longest-priced winner
40-1 Kearney (1980)

Shortest-priced winner
1-6 Black Caviar (2012)

Most successful trainer
5 wins: **Vincent O'Brien**
Welsh Saint (1970), Saritamer (1974), Swingtime (1975), Thatching (1979), College Chapel (1993)

Most successful jockey
9 wins: **Lester Piggott**
Right Boy (1958, 1959), Tin Whistle (1960), El Gallo (1963), Mountain Call (1968), Welsh Saint (1970), Saritamer (1974), Thatching (1979), College Chapel (1993)

*All figures since 1946

Most successful owners
2 wins: **Giles Loder**
Abadan (1950), Blood Test (1953)

Stanhope Joel
Matador (1957), Bun Penny (1961)

Geoffrey Gilbert
Right Boy (1958 & 1959)

Charles St George
El Gallo (1963), Saritamer (1974)

Robert Sangster
Thatching (1979), Committed (1984)

Khalid Abdullah
Danehill (1989), Expert Eye (2018)

Maktoum Al Maktoum
Great Commotion (1990), Royal Applause (1997)

Hamdan Al Maktoum
Atraf (1996), Malhub (2002)

4.20 Diamond Jubilee Stakes

Key trends
- ▶ *No older than six, 10/10*
- ▶ *Adjusted RPR of at least 127, 9/10*
- ▶ *Group or Listed winner over 6f, 9/10*
- ▶ *Top-three finish within last two starts, 9/10*
- ▶ *Trained in Britain or Ireland, 8/10*

Other factors
- ▶ *Only four winners had scored earlier in the season*
- ▶ *Three winners had run in the race the year before, finishing 278*
- ▶ *Six winners contested the Duke of York Stakes, in which they finished 035256*
- ▶ *Duke of York winners finished 29420*
- ▶ *Five winners had contested a previous Royal Ascot (one won, one placed and three unplaced)*

Merchant Navy and Ryan Moore after last year's victory

Story of the last ten years

	FORM	WINNER	AGE & WGT	Adj RPR	SP	TRAINER	BEST RPR LAST 12 MONTHS (RUNS SINCE)
18	1-331	**Merchant Navy** D	4 9-3	131-8	4-1	Aidan O'Brien (IRE)	won Curragh Gp2 (6f) (0)
17	121-5	**The Tin Man** CD	5 9-3	132-5	9-2	James Fanshawe	won Champions Sprint Gp1 (6f) (1)
16	112-5	**Twilight Son** D	4 9-3	132T	7-2	Henry Candy	2nd Champions Sprint Gp1 (6f) (1)
15	33-32	**Undrafted** D	5 9-3	127-8	14-1	Wesley Ward (USA)	3rd Breeders' Cup Turf Sprint Gd1 (6½f) (2)
14	210-1	**Slade Power** CD	5 9-4	131T	7-2f	Eddie Lynam (IRE)	won Curragh Gp3 (6f) (0)
13	130-2	**Lethal Force**	4 9-4	128-6	11-1	Clive Cox	2nd Duke of York Stakes Gp2 (6f) (0)
12	11111	**Black Caviar** D	6 9-1	143T	1-6f	Peter Moody (AUS)	won Flemington Gp1 (5f) (2)
11	27-02	**Society Rock** CD	4 9-4	127-3	25-1	James Fanshawe	2nd Golden Jubilee Stakes Gp1 (6f) (3)
10	-4135	**Starspangledbanner** D, BF	4 9-4	130-5	13-2j	Aidan O'Brien (IRE)	won Caulfield Gp1 (1m) (4)
09	128-7	**Art Connoisseur** CD	3 8-11	116-20	20-1	Michael Bell	2nd Phoenix Stakes Gp1 (6f) (2)

WINS-RUNS 3yo 1-3-13, 4yo 5-10-54, 5yo 3-5-42, 6yo+ 1-2-46 **FAVOURITES** -£0.58

TRAINERS IN THIS RACE (w-pl-r) Aidan O'Brien 2-1-8, James Fanshawe 2-2-7, Henry Candy 1-1-4, Wesley Ward 1-2-4, Charlie Hills 0-0-2, Andrew Balding 0-0-3, Charlie Appleby 0-0-2, John Gosden 0-0-1, Richard Hannon 0-0-2, Roger Charlton 0-0-6

FATE OF FAVOURITES 4101212430 **POSITION OF WINNER IN MARKET** 9101616322

THIS is one of the big handicap sprints of the Flat season, with close on 30 runners charging down the straight in a hotly contested 6f race.

Many punters will focus on the draw but recent runnings suggest the winner can come from anywhere on the track, often depending more on where the pace is. Last year the winner came from stall 16, while three of the first six were drawn in the 20s and two had single-digit stalls.

Even though only one favourite has won since 2005, seven of the 13 winners since then have come from the first four in the market. The class factor has been important, with nine of those 13 winners no more than 2lb off top-rated on Racing Post Ratings.

Winners have tended to

Key trends

▶ *Distance winner, 10/10*
▶ *Within 7lb of RPR top-rated, 10/10*
▶ *Officially rated between 95 and 106, 10/10*
▶ *No more than four runs that season, 9/10 (two winners were making their reappearance)*
▶ *Aged four or five, 8/10*
▶ *Top-four finish last time out, 8/10*
▶ *Carried no more than 9st 3lb, 7810*
▶ *Won over 7f, 7/10*
▶ *Won in Class 1 or 2 company, 6/10*

Other factors

▶ *Four winners were drawn between 12 and 22, three in one to 11 and three between 23 and 31*
▶ *Five winners were top or joint top-rated*
▶ *Five winners had won or placed in a field of at least 18 runners*

come from a narrow weights range, from 8st 12lb to 9st 3lb, although last year Bacchus won off 9st 6lb (Dandy Boy, the last 33-1 winner before him, had 9st 8lb in 2012).

The importance of getting into the race on the right sort of handicap mark is evident in the fact that only two of the last 13 winners had won that season, although nine had achieved a top-four finish last time out. Seven had gone up in the handicap that season (only three had dropped), so it is important to have shown a good level of form.

Big-field experience is also important, with eight of the last 13 winners having won or been placed in a field of 18 runners or more.

Newmarket stables have the best long-term record but northern trainers have done well recently, winning three of the last six runnings.

	FORM	WINNER		AGE & WGT	OR	SP	TRAINER	BEST RPR LAST 12 MONTHS (RUNS SINCE)
18	5314-	**Bacchus**	D	4 9-6	105-6	33-1	Brian Meehan	won Newmarket Class 2 hcap (6f) (1)
17	7-304	**Out Do**	D	8 8-13	99-2	25-1	David O'Meara	3rd Ascot Class 2 hcap (5f) (7)
16	40-70	**Outback Traveller**	C, D	5 9-1	100T	10-1	Robert Cowell	4th Ascot Class 2 hcap (7f) (3)
15	413-2	**Interception**	D	5 9-3	102-6	10-1	David Lanigan	2nd Haydock Listed (6f) (0)
14	50-22	**Baccarat**	D, BF	5 9-2	105T	9-1	Richard Fahey	2nd York Class 2 hcap (6f) (0)
13	56142	**York Glory**	D	5 9-2	100T	14-1	Kevin Ryan	2nd York Class 2 hcap (5f) (0)
12	-5992	**Dandy Boy**	C, D	6 9-8	106-7	33-1	David Marnane (IRE)	2nd Curragh hcap (1m) (0)
11	230-2	**Deacon Blues**	D	4 8-13	98-1	15-2	James Fanshawe	2nd Ascot Class 3 hcap (6f) (0)
10	1316/	**Laddies Poker Two**	CD, BF	5 8-11	95T	9-2f	Jeremy Noseda	Seasonal debut (0)
09	22-11	**High Standing** (5ex)	D	4 8-12	96T	6-1	William Haggas	won Goodwood Class 2 hcap (6f) (0)

WINS-RUNS 3yo 0-0-1, 4yo 3-12-90, 5yo 5-7-66, 6yo+ 2-11-111 **FAVOURITES** -£4.50

FATE OF FAVOURITES 0100005282 **POSITION OF WINNER IN MARKET** 2120644400

5.35 Queen Alexandra Stakes

THIS is the longest race of the week at two and three-quarter miles – indeed, the longest run under Flat racing rules – and one of the best loved, with just one of its traditional aspects being that it always closes the meeting.

With fewer out-and-out stayers in Flat yards nowadays, this race is more open to being won by a trainer better known for jump racing. Multiple champion jumps trainers Nicky Henderson and Willie Mullins (twice) figure on the roll of honour in the past ten years (as they do in other staying races at the meeting), along with Mullins' great Irish rival Gordon Elliott (twice in the last three years) and Gary Moore.

Five of the six winners from those yards had been

Key trends

▶ *Officially rated 90-plus, 10/10*
▶ *Drawn nine or higher, 8/10*
▶ *Adjusted RPR at least 113, 8/10 (exceptions hurdlers)*
▶ *Contested a Group or Listed race since last season, 8/10*
▶ *Aged five to seven, 7/10 (all three exceptions older)*
▶ *Rated within 7lb of RPR top-rated, 7/10*
▶ *Top-six finish in race over 2m2f-plus, 7/10*

Other factors

▶ *Only two winners had scored that season*

running over jumps during the winter and each one of that quintet had run at one of the big spring jumps festivals at Cheltenham, Aintree and Punchestown. Swingkeel, the 2011 winner, had been tried unsuccessfully over hurdles in the winter with Nigel Twiston-Davies

before returning to John Dunlop to win this race.

Mullins has the best record with figures of 08114032260 since 2010. He did the Ascot Stakes/Queen Alexandra double with Simenon at the 2012 meeting and went close in 2017 when Thomas Hobson won the first leg but was beaten into second here. Baddam also did the double in 2006 for Mick Channon.

Aidan O'Brien runners have to be noted. He won in 2008 with Honolulu and his only two runners since then have been placed. Other Flat trainers to watch are Mark Johnston (won in 2015 and 2017) and Andrew Balding (won in 2013 and had the third last year).

Most winners are prominent in the market, with nothing bigger than Commissioned (12-1 in 2016) since 2004.

Story of the last ten years

	FORM	WINNER	AGE & WGT	Adj RPR	SP	TRAINER	BEST RPR LAST 12 MONTHS (RUNS SINCE)
18	5668-	**Pallasator** C	9 9-2	124-1	11-2	Gordon Elliott (IRE)	6th Deauville Gp2 (1m7f) (1)
17	95-25	**Oriental Fox** CD	9 9-5	117-10	10-1	Mark Johnston	2nd Newmarket Class 2 hcap (1m6f) (1)
16	211/	**Commissioned**	6 9-2	113-11	12-1	Gordon Elliott (IRE)	Seasonal debut (0)
15	3756-	**Oriental Fox**	7 9-2	120-1	4-1	Mark Johnston	6th Northumberland Plate hcap (2m) (0)
14	321-5	**Pique Sous**	7 9-2	108-18	11-4	Willie Mullins (IRE)	won Leopardstown hcap (1m6f) (1)
13	525-5	**Chiberta King**	7 9-2	119T	8-1	Andrew Balding	5th Goodwood Gp2 (2m) (3)
12	350-1	**Simenon** C	5 9-2	119-7	11-4f	Willie Mullins (IRE)	won Ascot Class 2 hcap (2m4f) (0)
11	30-06	**Swingkeel**	6 9-2	113-5	11-2	John Dunlop	3rd Salisbury Class 2 (1m6f) (3)
10	112/5	**Bergo**	7 9-2	106-6	10-1	Gary Moore	5th Newbury Class 1 Listed (1m5½f) (0)
09	541-1	**Caracciola**	12 9-7	116T	6-1	Nicky Henderson	won Cesarewitch Handicap (2m2f) (1)

WINS-RUNS: 4yo 0-8-36, 5yo 1-2-25, 6yo+ 9-10-94 **FAVOURITES:** -£6.25

TRAINERS IN THIS RACE (w-pl-r) Willie Mullins 2-3-11, Gordon Elliott 2-0-2, Mark Johnston 2-0-4, Andrew Balding 1-1-5, Aidan O'Brien 0-2-2, Alan King 0-0-4, Charlie Appleby 0-0-2, Mick Channon 0-0-2, Hughie Morrison 0-0-4

FATE OF FAVOURITES 4621244326 **POSITION OF WINNER IN MARKET** 5521423643

THE DRAW

Racing Post betting editor Keith Melrose crunches the numbers on the Ascot draw

AT NO other meeting is the draw pored over as much as it is at Royal Ascot. Most of the other courses that stage big fixtures come with established biases or otherwise the meetings come late enough in the season that raw form study detains punters for much longer.

It is different here. For a start, this is the Flat season's adolescence: we are only a couple of weeks on from the Derby and still four months away from British Champions Day. The best formlines of the season are only just developing and you may not yet have heard of the St Leger winner.

Then there is the track itself. The round course is galloping, at just less than 1m6f to a circuit, with long straights and tight bends. The straight course is one of the longest in the country and hosts a majority (16) of the 30 races over the five days.

Ascot is a track that theoretically offers little in the way of a draw bias, so does it deserve all the scrutiny? There is no way to find out that does not involve heaping on a little more.

Draw analysis lends itself especially well to measuring the percentage of rivals beaten by all runners. While the graphic on pages 100-101 helpfully illustrates winners and placed runners, the extent to which an unfavoured group is disadvantaged is fully borne out only by inspection of the field as a whole.

All races at the royal meeting since 2014 were considered and thereafter broken down by course (round or straight), then by year.

What emerged straight

Expert analysis

away on the round course was its outstanding fairness. Taken either across the sample or in individual years, a horse drawn in stalls 18 to 22 (the latter being the maximum allowed) can expect to fare every bit as well as one drawn in stalls one to five.

The clues as to why this is have probably been covered already. A galloping track with no round-course races run over short of 1m (four of the 14 during Royal Ascot are over 1m6f+) is unlikely to throw up a strong bias. Still, it is worth noting that it holds for even the highest stalls.

The real conundrum is the straight course. Biases undoubtedly exist within races – all of us will have backed one on the 'wrong' side in the Royal Hunt Cup – but predicting them can be very difficult.

The headline figures generated on the straight course over the past five years add little clarity. At a push it could be argued that those drawn in stall 22 or higher (the maximum field size on the straight course is 33) have a marginal edge (51.4 per cent of rivals beaten) over those drawn in the middle third (49.8 per cent) or lower third (50.2 per cent).

The year-by-year figures shed a bit more light. In the past three years, an obvious bias is difficult to detect. In 2015, however, there was a significant bias towards the low-numbered stalls, which outperformed middle stalls by eight percentage points and high ones by 18, while in 2014 it was more or less exactly the other way round.

Observation is one thing, but is there a way to use this information to predict? It is clear that any bias on Ascot's straight course is one of conditions, whether it be ground, pace or the self-fulfilling prophecy of perception – if riders believe one path is 'quicker', more horses will end up there. More pace and more cover means better chances; as in the wild, there is safety in numbers.

The straight-course races on day one of Royal Ascot have been the Queen ▶

THE DRAW

Anne, Coventry, King's Stand and, until 2018, the Windsor Castle.

Looking at the horses to have featured prominently in those races in 2014 and 2015, it can be seen that the Queen Anne, which normally provides the smallest field of the four, is not especially helpful. Nor is the Coventry, which is a little more surprising.

By the time we reach the King's Stand, the ultimate trend can just about be made out. Take the results in the Windsor Castle, which provided by far the biggest field in both years, and it can be seen that the trend for the week is being set.

Whatever its cause, it seems that any perceived bias on the straight track is spotted early in the week and defines how races pan out for the rest of the meeting.

The problem is obvious, however: the Windsor

Castle, the supposed skeleton key, has been moved to the end of Wednesday's card and the last race on Tuesday is now the Wolferton Stakes, over 1m2f on the round course.

In future, the Windsor Castle's job may be filled by the Queen Mary, race one on Wednesday, which in the five years covered has provided field sizes of 22, 23, 17, 20 and 21. It is not ideal to wait another day, but at least it offers two and a half hours to potentially revise our view on the Hunt Cup!

Let us not lose sight of the other major finding. In the past three years, there has been no huge bias on the straight course over the course of the week. The best advice is to bet as you please, use the draw advisedly and primarily through the lens of pace, while keeping a close eye on the King's Stand and Queen Mary results.

Runners pull up after last year's Royal Hunt Cup – one of the races where the draw is scrutinised most closely

CONCLUSIONS

- The round course is remarkably fair. Even if you fancy one drawn in the 20s, don't fret
- The straight course is not as riddled with biases as it perhaps once was. Follow the pace
- In years when a straight-course bias does emerge, it becomes apparent in the first day or so. Watch out for the King's Stand and Queen Mary setting the tone

EFFECT OF DRAW AT ROYAL ASCOT

Straight-course races with 16+ runners (2014-18)

Top 4 finishers shown by draw section
■ Low ■ Middle ■ High

2014

Winners from each section: H7 M2 L0
Placed horses from each section: H20 M13 L3

Race	Distance	Going	1st	2nd	3rd	4th
King's Stand	5f	Good	M	L	M	M
Windsor Castle	5f	Good	H	H	H	L
Jersey	7f	GF	H	L	M	H
Queen Mary	5f	GF	M	H	H	M
Royal Hunt Cup	1m	GF	H	M	H	H
Sandringham	1m	GF	H	H	H	H
Britannia	1m	GF	H	H	M	H
Albany	6f	GF	H	M	M	M
Wokingham	6f	GF	H	M	M	H

2015

Winners from each section: H4 M5 L2
Placed horses from each section: H11 M17 L16

Race	Distance	Going	1st	2nd	3rd	4th
Coventry	6f	GF	M	M	L	M
King's Stand	5f	GF	L	L	M	H
Windsor Castle	5f	GF	L	L	M	L
Jersey	7f	GF	M	M	L	L
Queen Mary	5f	GF	H	L	L	H
Royal Hunt Cup	1m	GF	M	M	L	H
Sandringham	1m	GF	H	L	L	H
Britannia	1m	GF	M	L	H	L
Albany	6f	GF	H	H	M	M
Commonwealth Cup	6f	GF	M	H	M	L
Wokingham	6f	GF	H	H	L	M

2016

Race	Distance	Going	1st	2nd	3rd	4th
Coventry	6f	Soft	H	L	M	L
King's Stand	5f	Soft	M	H	M	H
Windsor Castle	5f	Soft	L	L	M	H
Jersey	7f	Soft	M	H	L	L
Queen Mary	5f	Soft	H	M	L	M
Royal Hunt Cup	1m	Soft	L	H	H	M
Sandringham	1m	Soft	H	H	H	M
Britannia	1m	Soft	M	H	H	H
Albany	6f	GS	H	L	H	H
Wokingham	6f	GS	H	M	H	L

2017

Race	Distance	Going	1st	2nd	3rd	4th
Coventry	6f	GF	M	H	L	M
King's Stand	5f	GF	H	L	M	L
Queen Anne	1m	GF	L	M	M	H
Windsor Castle	5f	GF	M	L	L	M
Jersey	7f	GF	M	H	H	M
Queen Mary	5f	GF	H	H	H	M
Royal Hunt Cup	1m	GF	M	H	M	M
Sandringham	1m	GF	M	H	H	M
Britannia	1m	GF	L	L	L	H
Norfolk	5f	GF	L	H	H	L
Albany	6f	GF	M	L	H	H
Diamond Jubilee	6f	GF	L	M	H	M
Wokingham	6f	GF	L	L	M	M

2018

Race	Distance	Going	1st	2nd	3rd	4th
Coventry	6f	GF	H	L	L	M
Jersey	7f	GF	M	M	M	M
Queen Mary	5f	GF	H	M	H	M
Royal Hunt Cup	1m	GF	H	M	M	M
Sandringham	1m	GF	L	M	M	H
Britannia	1m	GF	M	H	L	M
Albany	6f	GF	H	H	L	L
Commonwealth Cup	6f	GF	L	H	M	M
Windsor Castle	5f	GF	H	H	L	L
Wokingham	6f	GF	M	L	H	L

THE HANDICAPS

Dave Orton looks at factors to consider in the handicaps

ROYAL ASCOT now features a big handicap as the fifth race on each card and for some punters this is the daily puzzle they enjoy above all, as they try to untangle the lines of form and weigh up which horses have the most untapped potential.

It is, of course, easy to be attracted to horses who won on their previous outing. However, relying on such runners in handicaps has proved a rapid way to deplete a betting bank in recent seasons.

The overall record of last-time-out winners since 2016 is 10-138 (7%) for a level-stake loss of 60.25pt. Last year four such horses obliged out of 57 candidates – interestingly all of them in the three-year-olds-only handicaps – but in 2017 punters who followed the winning form got stung, with no winner from 39 runners.

Following specific stables has often paid off. A prime example is the week's first handicap, the Ascot Stakes, run over a marathon distance of 2m4f. Since the turn of the millennium, 14 renewals have gone to predominantly jumps trainers. Irish-trained runners have taken six of the past seven, with Willie Mullins responsible for four

of those. Ireland's champion jumps trainer even saddled a 1-3-4-5 in last year's edition.

One to note in the 1m4f handicaps is Mark Johnston, who has six wins in the King George V (the latest was Baghdad at 9-1 last year) and three in the Duke of Edinburgh. Other trainers with good records in handicaps include Jamie Osborne (who has won two of the last ten runnings of the big mile handicaps, the Royal Hunt Cup and Britannia), Hughie Morrison (a track record of success, plus a second and third at double-figure odds last year) and Roger Charlton.

Having the benefit of some previous Ascot form can be important, especially in handicaps for the older horses. Remember Ascot is a sand-based turf track, so

horses who have prospered on the all-weather often come to the fore. That was borne out in last year's Hunt Cup won by the Irish-trained Settle For Bay, who had rattled up a four-timer on Dundalk's Polytrack the previous winter.

Handicaps place most significance on the importance of the draw simply because they attract the biggest number of runners. On the straight track at up to a mile, the most important factor is

where the early pace will come from, so identifying likely front-runners is key.

At last year's meeting those who stayed towards the far side in both the Hunt Cup and Britannia struggled to make any sort of an impact. However, in the 6f Wokingham on the final day the far side had much more of a say, with the first two racing in the group that went over there, highlighting no real bias on the ground.

Races on the round course are always contested at a searing pace, and interestingly last season those drawn in double figures held a significant advantage. That was often down to avoiding a troubled passage as things became tight in the home straight.

For example, in the 1m4f King George V, six of the first eight finishers were berthed in double figures. The two drawn low in that group, First Eleven and Occupy, would have both finished closer but for troubled runs – the former being particularly unlucky.

With that in mind, the days of simply searching out a prominent racer drawn low in handicaps on the round course seem to be over.

The bigger operations are often responsible for shaping the betting market in handicaps at the meeting but Aidan O'Brien is just 1-15 since 2016 and John Gosden is 1-25 in the same period. Gosden's Dreamfield went off just 2-1 for the Wokingham last year but failed to repel 33-1 shot Bacchus by a neck.

That was a reminder of a valuable lesson: never be afraid to take a big price in handicaps at Royal Ascot.

Settle For Bay: Dundalk specialist lands last year's Hunt Cup in good style

FIVE OF THE BEST . . .

The Queen's daily presence at the races puts the 'Royal' into Royal Ascot. She first attended the meeting in 1945 at the age of 19 and has hardly missed a day in the intervening 74 years, enjoying 23 winners in the famous royal colours of purple body with gold braid, scarlet sleeves and black velvet cap with gold fringe. **Julian Muscat** *looks at the pick of her winners . . .*

AUREOLE 1954 HARDWICKE

It wasn't uncommon for Aureole, a horse with his own mind, to drop his rider while out at exercise in Newmarket. The 1953 Derby runner-up was on his best behaviour here, however, as he regained the lead from French challenger Janitor well inside the final furlong to prevail by a short head under jockey Eph Smith.

Previously winner of the Coronation Cup, Aureole subsequently landed the King George VI and Queen Elizabeth Stakes despite losing ground at the start. His exploits in 1954 were largely responsible for the Queen becoming champion owner.

ALMERIA 1957 RIBBLESDALE

A leading fancy for the 1957 Oaks, Almeria pulled a muscle and was unable to make it to Epsom. It mattered little from the Queen's perspective; she won the Oaks anyway with Carrozza. Almeria, for her part, demonstrated her prowess by winning the Ribblesdale Stakes.

Indeed, Almeria ended the season with a higher official rating than Carrozza. She went on to win the Yorkshire Oaks and Park Hill Stakes before chasing home Ballymoss in the following year's King George VI and Queen Elizabeth Stakes.

PALL MALL 1957 NEW (NORFOLK)

The 1950s was a golden decade for the Queen at Royal Ascot. She had 11 winners, among them Pall Mall's New Stakes triumph. Trained by Cecil Boyd-Rochfort, the royal colt won by a length from Troubadour with Harry Carr aboard.

While Pall Mall's triumph wasn't in itself a seminal victory, the colt went on to earn the distinction of becoming his owner's first homebred Classic winner when he landed the 2,000 Guineas the following year. He also won the Lockinge Stakes twice.

HOPEFUL VENTURE 1968 HARDWICKE

A colt by Aureole, Hopeful Venture would probably have won the 1967 King Edward VII Stakes but for stumbling badly in the home straight. However, he made handsome amends when landing the odds in the Hardwicke Stakes 12 months later.

Hopeful Venture was a contemporary of 2,000 Guineas and Derby winner Royal Palace at Noel Murless's Warren Place Stables.

The two horses monopolised middle-distance races as four-year-olds in 1968, when Hopeful Venture also won the Grand Prix de Saint-Cloud.

Royal winners

THE QUEEN'S 23 ROYAL ASCOT WINNERS

YEAR	RACE	HORSE	JOCKEY
1953	Royal Hunt Cup	**CHOIR BOY**	Doug Smith
1954	Hardwicke Stakes	**AUREOLE**	Eph Smith
	Rous Memorial Stakes	**LANDAU**	Gordon Richards
1955	King George V Stakes	**JARDINIERE**	Doug Smith
1956	Royal Hunt Cup	**ALEXANDER**	Harry Carr
1957	Ribblesdale Stakes	**ALMERIA**	Harry Carr
	New Stakes	**PALL MALL**	Harry Carr
1958	Rous Memorial Stakes	**SNOW CAT**	Eph Smith
	King Edward VII Stakes	**RESTORATION**	Harry Carr
1959	St James's Palace Stakes	**ABOVE SUSPICION**	Harry Carr
	King Edward VII Stakes	**PINDARI**	Lester Piggott
1961	Coronation Stakes	**AIMING HIGH**	Lester Piggott
1968	Hardwicke Stakes	**HOPEFUL VENTURE**	Sandy Barclay
1970	Ascot Stakes	**MAGNA CARTA**	Geoff Lewis
1979	Queen's Vase	**BUTTRESS**	Willie Carson
	Ribblesdale Stakes	**EXPANSIVE**	Willie Carson
1992	Royal Hunt Cup	**COLOUR SERGEANT**	David Harrison
1995	Ribblesdale Stakes	**PHANTOM GOLD**	Frankie Dettori
1999	Duke of Edinburgh Stks	**BLUEPRINT**	Gary Stevens
2008	Chesham Stakes	**FREE AGENT** Richard Hughes	
2012	Queen's Vase	**ESTIMATE** Ryan Moore	
2013	Gold Cup	**ESTIMATE** Ryan Moore	
2016	Hardwicke Stakes	**DARTMOUTH** Olivier Peslier	

ESTIMATE 2012 QUEEN'S VASE, 2013 GOLD CUP

Estimate is the only horse owned by the Queen to win twice at Royal Ascot. She landed the Queen's Vase in Diamond Jubilee year and the meeting's signature race, the Gold Cup, 12 months later. Trained by Sir Michael Stoute, she was ridden on both occasions by Ryan Moore. Estimate's Gold Cup neck defeat of Simenon generated euphoric scenes – "The crowd's reaction was probably unlike anything else I have ever heard on a track," Moore said – and the Queen later told Stoute the Gold Cup was the race she had most wanted to win.

One of the most magnificent sights of a day at Royal Ascot is the royal procession, which brings the Queen and her guests along the straight mile in horse-drawn carriages, parading in front of the vast crowds before turning under the grandstand and into the parade ring

The royal procession did not start until 1825 during the reign of King George IV. Initially it took place on only one day of the meeting before it was extended to all days in 1919, in celebration of victory in the First World War.

The procession starts not by carriage but by car. The Queen and her guests leave Windsor Castle at 1.35pm and are driven by car to the Ascot Gate of Windsor Great Park, where they transfer to four horse-drawn carriages.

Each landau carriage carries four people, with the Queen at the head of

the group. The carriages are pulled by Windsor greys and bays, mainly Cleveland bays, who are trained as carriage horses from the age of four and work for approximately 15 years.

The procession along the straight mile starts at 2pm precisely and a different path is chosen each day, to protect the ground. As the procession reaches the grandstand, the national anthem is played by a guards band.

In 1929 King George V was absent with illness, in 1964 and again in 1971 there were cancellations due to

Grand entrance: The carriages arrive in the parade ring after the Queen leads the procession down the course (inset)

bad weather, and political events stopped the spectacle in 1970 when there was a general election on the Thursday and in 2001 for the state opening of parliament.

FASHION

The Ascot team with the latest trends and tips for a stylish royal meeting

*R*oyal Ascot is one of the major events of the summer social season and fashion plays a huge part for racegoers. Ascot Racecourse has launched its eighth annual Style Guide – in association with luxury cruise brand Cunard – featuring beautiful jumpsuits and trouser suits, elegant hats and statement bows.

Ascot worked with renowned stylist Prue White on the curation of the 2019 looks and has included a selection of geometric and floral print dresses and jumpsuits in soft pastel tones oozing timeless elegance.

Ascot has curated looks featuring designers Emilia Wickstead, Zimmerman, Victoria Beckham, Simone Rocha, Jimmy Choo, Delpozo, Erdem, Katya Katya, Suzannah and Mary Katrantzou, with support from milliners including Philip Treacy OBE, Awon Golding, Stephen Jones OBE, Jane Taylor, Edwina Ibbotson and Rachel Trevor Morgan.

Last year saw an increase of racegoers wearing trouser suits and jumpsuits and once again these are set to be part of the summer fashion highlights. The inclusion of jumpsuits as part of the official Royal Ascot Dress Code recognises the fashion-forward taste of racegoers and reflects Ascot's awareness of seasonal trends.

What's hot this summer

FASHION

Picking your outfit for Royal Ascot may take months of planning and shopping but when you finally find the perfect outfit there's no better feeling. The official Royal Ascot Dress Code ensures all racegoers are able to feel comfortable and relaxed in their outfits. So whether you prefer a floaty dress or jumpsuit, there's an option for you to look and feel your best

Exude effortless elegance with ever-popular floral wide-leg jumpsuits teamed with neutral accessories

Monochrome is back as a key trend. The delicate detail on this classic dress is divine and is easily styled with dainty jewellery and black and white accessories, and a stylish wide-brim hat adds the finishing touch to this elegant look

The looks

Head-to-toe white, a graceful look perfect for the Royal Enclosure. At Royal Ascot your hat is your crowning glory, so choose a style that elevates your all-white ensemble

Bright colours are a hot trend. Sometimes a little pop of colour can go a long way and this dress is beautifully stylish. The stripe bow detail complements the base of the dress and hat

FASHION

Award-winning milliner Awon Golding gives her view

How long have you been supplying hats for Royal Ascot?
I'm part of the Royal Ascot Millinery Collective, sponsored by Fenwick, for a second year in 2019 but I've been making hats for clients heading to the royal meeting for nearly a decade now.

What's in this year?
Boaters are definitely still happening – they're so elegantly classic in shape and a wide brim can be a really flattering shape for Royal Ascot.

I've designed a black and white boater for the 2019 Royal Ascot Millinery Collective which is really chic and has a playful feel with an ornate bow and bright pink pom-pom hat pin. Coral and emerald seem to be popular colours and bows are a big trend.

Crescent headbands have really come to the forefront of millinery fashion this year too.

What has demand been like this year?
Fantastic. People have definitely thought about their hats earlier this year.

'There's a real range as different styles appeal to different ages'

Millinery featured heavily on the spring/summer catwalk shows with Chanel, Moschino and Erdem all featuring hats – this has definitely helped to put millinery at the forefront of people's minds.

People have been buying the spring/summer collection from the start of the year when it went on sale through my website and in-store at Fenwick on Bond Street.

Who are your clients?
The majority are British, although I have a fair few from Australia and America too. In terms of age, there's a real range as different styles appeal to different ages. A lot of my younger clients are looking for more fun and colourful styles, whereas my more mature clients lean toward classic shapes and larger brims. The wonderful thing about millinery is that each design can be created or customised to suit an individual's personality and taste.

How important is Royal Ascot to your business?
Very important – it's an event that focuses the millinery industry and is a

great showcase for designers. June also coincides with the wedding season and I think people have become more open to wearing a hat to an occasion. Royal Ascot acts as a shop window and inspires the creations to come for the following year.

• Awon Golding Millinery
www.awongolding.com
07805 577 376
@awongolding on Instagram

FASHION

ROYAL ENCLOSURE

◀ A dress below the knee is encouraged in the Royal Enclosure. British designer Suzannah adds a bow detail to this dress, which can be easily styled with a classic hat

QUEEN ANNE ENCLOSURE

▶ Monochrome never goes out of style; the simple silhouette of this Emilio de la Morena dress means it can be easily teamed with a striking headpiece for the Queen Anne Enclosure

What to wear

WINDSOR ENCLOSURE

This exquisite and colourful Rixo dress is a great summer look for a day at the races

VILLAGE ENCLOSURE

▲ This striking Mother of Pearl jumpsuit is the perfect dress alternative for Royal Ascot

FASHION

Style Guide
THE KEY POINTS

ROYAL ENCLOSURE

Ladies
- Formal daywear is a requirement
- Dresses and skirts should fall just above the knee or longer
- Dresses and tops should have straps of one inch or greater
- Trouser suits and jumpsuits are welcome – trouser suits should be full length, of matching material and colour; jumpsuits should fall below the knee, following the regulations for dresses
- Hats should be worn. Headpieces must have a solid base of four inches or more

Gentlemen
- Black or grey morning dress must be worn
- With a waistcoat and tie (no cravats or bow ties)
- A black or grey top hat
- Black shoes with socks

QUEEN ANNE ENCLOSURE

Ladies
- Ladies are required to dress in a manner as befits a formal occasion
- A hat, headpiece or fascinator should be worn at all times
- Strapless or sheer dresses and tops are not permitted
- Trouser suits must be full-length and jumpsuits should fall below the knee
- Shorts are not permitted

Gentlemen
- A full-length suit with a collared shirt and tie must be worn (no bow ties or cravats)
- Jackets and trousers must be of matching colour and pattern
- Socks must be worn and should cover the ankle

VILLAGE ENCLOSURE

Ladies
- Ladies are required to dress in a manner as

befits a formal occasion
- A hat, headpiece or fascinator should be worn at all times
- Strapless or sheer dresses and tops are not permitted
- Trouser suits must be full-length and jumpsuits should fall below the knee
- Shorts are not permitted

Gentlemen
- A jacket, full-length trousers, collared shirt and tie must be worn
- Ties, bow ties and cravats can be worn
- Socks must be worn and should cover the ankle
- Jeans, trainers and shorts are not permitted

WINDSOR ENCLOSURE

Ladies
- Suggestions: Dress in smart daywear, with a hat or fascinator

Gentlemen
- Suggestions: A jacket, collared shirt and full-length trousers

'If you're feeling bold, start with your hat. Find something you love and that flatters your face – both colouring and shape – and build your outfit from there'
Prue White, stylist

Six items you will never regret having in your handbag for Royal Ascot

- Your signature lipstick
- Loose powder compact
- Hand fan
- Safety pins
- Hand sanitiser
- Purse

What Royal Ascot does not want to see

Ladies
- No fascinators in the Royal Enclosure
- No midriffs uncovered in the Royal, Queen Anne and Village Enclosures
- No shorts in the Royal, Queen Anne and Village Enclosures
- No strapless or sheer dresses and tops in the Royal, Queen Anne and Village Enclosures

Gentlemen
- No novelty waistcoats and ties, unless of a patriotic nature (for example, your national flag) in the Royal Enclosure
- No customisation of top hats (with, for example, coloured ribbons or bands) in the Royal Enclosure
- No jeans or trainers in the Queen Anne and Village Enclosures
- No chinos in the Queen Anne Enclosure

And finally . . .
- In addition to the specific guidance of the Dress Code, fancy dress, novelty and branded or promotional clothing is not permitted on site

Hand Crafted Luxury

Herbert Johnson manufacturers of fine bespoke headwear originally since 1786
Handcrafted in our London workshops to the highest quality
Leading restorations for vintage hats to retain heritage and value

N & COUNTRY   MILITARY   CIVILIAN   EQUESTRIAN

London Store
7 Piccadilly Arcade, off Jermyn Street, London SW1Y 6NH
0207 409 7277 | piccadilly@swaine-adeney-brigg.co.uk | www.swaineadeneybrigg.com

Superstar ready for the

EPSOM'S loss was Ascot's gain when it was announced in mid-May that Enable would bypass the Coronation Cup and instead head to the royal meeting for her seasonal debut in the Prince of Wales's Stakes or the Hardwicke Stakes.

The superstar mare is one of the biggest attractions in Flat racing and her first appearance at Royal Ascot will be a major talking point, not least over the choice of race.

When it was announced she would go there rather than Epsom, Teddy Grimthorpe, racing manager to Khalid Abdullah, suggested the Group 1 Prince of Wales's, over a mile and a quarter, was the more likely of the two options.

He said: "In principle she'll run in the Prince of Wales's but we'll also be looking at the Hardwicke, so we're definitely not committing yet to one race over the other."

The Prince of Wales's is one of the jewels of Royal Ascot but Enable has not raced over 1m2f since her first start as a three-year-old in April 2017. She did not win that Newbury race, finishing third behind her briefly more highly regarded stablemate Shutter Speed, in the only defeat of her 11-race career.

Clearly she is an infinitely better racehorse now but taking on 1m2f specialists – even in a division lacking a standout potential champion this year – would be a big test.

The Hardwicke, down a notch at Group 2 and over her regular trip of 1m4f, would be a more comfortable target but lacks the kudos of the Prince of Wales's.

Ultimately the choice will be seen by connections as part of the long game, which is geared towards Enable's bid for a record third Prix de l'Arc de Triomphe victory in October. Last season injury

prevented her reappearance until September and there has been no rush to get her started this year, with all eyes focused on the autumn.

Equally she was hardy enough to stand a string of high-level races as a three-year-old, winning five Group 1s in a row in a four-month period from the Oaks in June to the Arc in October, and Gosden can be expected to produce her in

'The superstar mare is one of the biggest attractions in Flat racing and her first appearance at Royal Ascot will be a major talking point, not least over the choice of race'

Owner: Khalid Abdullah
Trainer: John Gosden

royal show

excellent shape at Royal
Ascot.

After the royal meeting she
is likely to return to Ascot in
search of a second King
George VI and Queen
Elizabeth Stakes victory.
Ascot's gain indeed, as they
might be her final runs in
Britain. We should treasure
her while we can.

STAR RATING
★ ★ ★ ★ ★

THERE is no more exciting sprinter around than Battaash and arguably none that can live with him when he generates his electrifying best.

This will be the five-year-old's third season of top-level sprinting and in each of the previous two campaigns he has produced dazzling performances that rank among the best of the past 20 years.

Explosive with a short fuse

At the end of the 2017 season he scorched home by four lengths in the Prix de l'Abbaye, achieving a Racing Post Rating of 128, and last year he went even higher with his RPR of 129 for

another four-length demolition, this time in the Group 2 King George Stakes at Goodwood.

The only other European-trained sprinters to reach that level since 2000 were

Battaash (blue cap, third left): one of the best sprinters of the past 20 years

Mozart in 2001 and Oasis Dream in 2003, and only Cracksman recorded a higher RPR in the 2018 European Flat season across all distances.

Yet there is hope for Battaash's potential rivals in the King's Stand Stakes because the explosiveness comes with a short fuse and he can sometimes be a damp squib. On his last two starts of 2018 he was fourth in the Nunthorpe Stakes and Abbaye, returning RPRs of 108 and 111 that put him around a stone and a half below his Goodwood form.

"I don't know what to make of it," said jockey Jim Crowley after the Nunthorpe, and favourite backers would have been equally nonplussed after that defeat at odds of 4-5 and the Abbaye loss at 11-10.

Battaash held it together pretty well in last year's King's Stand but still came up short, losing out by a length and three-quarters to Blue Point after leading most of the way.

"It's a hard track to make the running and you're there to be shot at," said Crowley. Ascot hasn't changed, though, and Battaash will have to show something different this year if he is to land his first Group 1 win since the 2017 Abbaye.

That is a long drought at the top level for one so talented. There would be no better place to hit top form again than Royal Ascot.

STAR RATING
★★★★★

The streetfighter with a wild side

Owner: Bjorn Nielsen
Trainer: John Gosden

THE winning machine known as Stradivarius will bid for a magnificent seventh straight victory when he goes for a second Gold Cup in what is shaping up as one of the best races of Royal Ascot 2019.

The race was tough enough last year, when barely a length separated John Gosden's talented stayer from Vazirabad and Torcedor in a dramatic finish, but this year's could be even more difficult with Melbourne Cup winner Cross Counter leading the opposition. On official ratings Stradivarius has only 2lb in hand over his main rival.

Even so, there is no doubt Stradivarius is the one to beat. He is undefeated since finishing third in the Long Distance Cup on Champions Day in 2017, having racked up five wins last year and another one on his reappearance this season in the Yorkshire Cup. The first four of his 2018 victories – in the Yorkshire Cup, Gold Cup, Goodwood Cup and Lonsdale Cup – earned him the £1m bonus for completing the Weatherbys Hamilton Stayers' Million in its inaugural year.

His second Yorkshire Cup success has set up another tilt at that huge prize but others in the hunt include Cross Counter and Dee Ex Bee, who have also won initial qualifying races. The Gold Cup will leave only one standing in the £1m bonus race, which adds extra spice to an already hot contest.

Another ingredient in the mix is Stradivarius's character, which brings a helping of jeopardy to each racecourse appearance. His biggest margin of victory in his six-race winning streak was three lengths and three of the victories were by less than a length, including this year's Yorkshire Cup by three-quarters of a length from Southern France.

"Stradivarius is the best stayer I've trained but he's never going to win by five lengths and show off – that's not his style," Gosden said at York. "It's like all of us, the older we get, the more we need galvanising."

Stradivarius needs no geeing up before his races, as we also saw at York. "He was roaring, shouting and slightly misbehaving [in the parade ring]," said Gosden. "He was in the nightclub when I was saddling him, but once he gets over being a stallion he goes out on the track and he's in a different zone. He's a streetfighter."

Gosden promised his scrapper would be more honed for the big bout at Ascot. "He was a little ring-rusty [at York], so he should come forward. He wasn't the polished, finished article but we hope to have that right at Royal Ascot."

Fighting talk indeed.

STAR RATING
★ ★ ★ ★ ★

'There is no doubt Stradivarius is the one to beat. He is undefeated since finishing third on Champions Day in 2017, having racked up five wins last year and another one on his reappearance this season in the Yorkshire Cup'

Exciting plans for Class act

THE Prix de l'Arc de Triomphe was perhaps the most exciting contest of the 2018 Flat season and, even though Sea Of Class came out just the wrong side of her tremendous duel with Enable, it was a race brimming with rich promise of even better to come this year.

Unraced as a juvenile, Sea Of Class was brilliantly progressive throughout her first season on the track. From an opening Racing Post Rating of 88 for a neck defeat on her debut as a three-year-old in a Newmarket mile maiden, she improved with every run to reach a high of 121 on RPR in her agonising short-neck

'A wide draw compromised her chance in the Arc, leaving her with just a little too much ground to make up in the home straight, but only the streetwise and more experienced Enable could stop her'

defeat by Enable less than six months later.

Along the way Sea Of Class recorded Group 1 victories in the Irish Oaks and Yorkshire Oaks, beating other high-class fillies such as Oaks winner Forever Together and star miler Laurens with an exhilarating hold-up style of running.

A wide draw compromised her chance in the Arc, leaving her with just a little too much ground to make up in the home straight, but only the streetwise and more experienced Enable could stop her.

With both fillies still in training, more battles are anticipated and the first of them could come in the Prince of Wales's Stakes – a mouthwatering prospect in one of the showpiece races of Royal Ascot.

Trainer William Haggas is relishing the prospect of testing Sea Of Class in the best company in her second season.

"I'm very keen to have a crack at the colts this year. It's a bit softly-softly to go for all the Group 1 races for fillies," he said.

"The other thing I want to do is bring her back in trip because I don't think she won any race last year because she

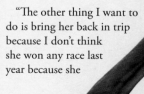

outgalloped them. I think she won because she was quicker than them."

Although the daughter of Sea The Stars stepped up to 1m4f for her three Group 1 assignments last season, she had won two Listed races over 1m2f and Haggas believes she could have been competitive against crack Japanese filly Almond Eye in the 1m1f Dubai Turf at Meydan in March.

"Sea Of Class would have been interesting in that nine-furlong race because I think she's quite similar [to Almond Eye]," he said. "She's got a turn of foot, so I really want to go for the Prince of Wales's."

STAR RATING

★★★★★

Melbourne Cup hero on the up

AT LAST year's royal meeting Cross Counter was just a handicapper – and a beaten one at that – but he went on to become one of the stars in an outstanding year for Godolphin and is now a genuine threat to Stradivarius in a mouthwatering Gold Cup.

Cross Counter had an official rating of 98 when he was fourth in last year's King

Owner: Godolphin
Trainer: Charlie Appleby

George V Handicap, but he has improved on all five subsequent runs and now stands on 118, just 2lb below the mark reached by Stradivarius in 2018.

The biggest moment for Cross Counter's connections was his historic win in last November's Melbourne Cup – a first for Godolphin and for a British-trained runner – and he stepped up another notch on his reappearance with victory in the Group 2 Dubai Gold Cup at Meydan in March.

The Dubai race is now one of the eight starting points for the Weatherbys Hamilton Stayers' Million – the £1m bonus if a horse wins one of those races and goes on to take the Gold Cup, the Goodwood Cup in July and the Lonsdale Cup at York in August – and that lucrative prize is clearly an attractive target after Stradivarius pulled off the feat last year.

Cross Counter was given time to rest in Dubai before arriving back in Britain in early May to be prepared for

the Gold Cup. He has yet to race beyond two miles but that is usually the case with Gold Cup newcomers and there is every hope his stamina will hold out.

The four-year-old's form lines are certainly strong. In last year's Gordon Stakes at Goodwood he was four and a half lengths clear of Dee Ex Bee – the Sagaro Stakes winner and a possible Gold Cup rival – and he was a head second in the Great Voltigeur Stakes at York behind stablemate Old Persian, who has gone on to land the Group 1 Dubai Sheema Classic.

With connections expecting more improvement, Cross Counter has a serious shot at gold.

STAR RATING
★ ★ ★ ★ ★

Blue flash goes for repeat victory

Owner: Godolphin
Trainer: Charlie Appleby

LAST year Blue Point upset the big two in the King's Stand Stakes, relegating Battaash and Lady Aurelia to minor roles with a commanding victory. Now, having proved emphatically that he belongs in sprinting's top rank, he returns as one to beat.

Royal victory over Battaash by a length and three-quarters was Blue Point's first Group 1 but he comes here after an excellent winter campaign in Dubai, capped by a second top-level success in the Al Quoz Sprint on World Cup night.

That certainly gives his form a better look than at this time last year. Back then he had been beaten in a Group 2 at Meydan in February (a race he won by five lengths this time) and finished last of nine in a Group 1 in Hong Kong, just seven weeks before Royal Ascot.

His overall form still entitled him to go off third favourite in the King's Stand and he rediscovered his spark

in great style, tracking Battaash from the off and forging past inside the final furlong with a determined run under William Buick.

That took his form figures at Ascot to 1311, with the only defeat coming on his previous visit to the royal meeting when he went down by little more than a length behind Caravaggio and Harry Angel in a red-hot edition of the Commonwealth Cup.

He ran to Racing Post Ratings of 117, 119, 119 and 123 in those four Ascot appearances, although his overall profile took a couple of dents last summer when he was only seventh in the

July Cup (RPR 108) and third in the Nunthorpe Stakes (109).

If that raised some doubt about his ability to maintain a high level of form, things looked different after a dominant winter campaign. He matched his best mark of 123 in a Meydan Group 3, with 121 on his two runs either side of that, and returns to his favourite track after a rest in Dubai's warm climate before arriving back in Britain in early May.

Sole Power in 2013-14 is the only sprinter to have won back-to-back King's Stands in the modern era but Buick is confident Blue Point has what it takes.

"It's great at the age of five he's showing everyone just how good he is and he's always shown us so much speed," the jockey said after the Al Quoz Sprint. "I remember riding him as a two-year-old and I'd never ridden a faster horse before he made his debut. He's developed into a top-class sprinter now."

STAR RATING
★★★★★

Fast track to the top

CALYX left one of the deepest impressions at Royal Ascot 2018 with his scorching victory in the Coventry Stakes and his return for this year's Commonwealth Cup looks set to be one of the most hotly anticipated events of the meeting.

A first step into Group 1 company has been long delayed for the John Gosden-trained colt, who took his record to two-from-two with his one-length victory over Advertise in the Group 2 Coventry. That appeared to put him on course for top-level honours before the end of his juvenile campaign but, while Advertise quickly graduated to Group 1 standard with victory in the Phoenix Stakes followed by second place behind Too Darn Hot in the Dewhurst Stakes, Calyx was sidelined by injury for the rest of the season.

Before that setback Calyx had been ante-post favourite for the 2,000 Guineas, such was the excitement after his Coventry triumph, and he was still no bigger than 8-1 for the season's first Classic until connections decided in late April that going straight for the Guineas after his long layoff would be asking too much of him.

Instead he returned to Ascot for the Group 3 Commonwealth Cup Trial over six furlongs on May 1 and it was as if he had never been away. Over the same

course and distance as the Coventry, and the same good to firm ground, he made light of his 11-month absence with a blistering four-length victory under Frankie Dettori.

Before the race there was talk of a miling campaign, with the St James's Palace Stakes mooted as the Royal Ascot target, but Calyx's performance changed the mood music, reigniting all the old excitement with a performance stamped with the hallmark of a potential top-class sprinter.

Gosden wasted no time in confirming the change of target, saying: "Frankie came back and said, 'John, he might be bred to be a miler but he likes to sprint', so all being well we'll be back here for the Commonwealth Cup."

The Ascot race, formerly known as the Pavilion Stakes, has a good recent pedigree as a launchpad for top-class sprinters, having been won by Limato in 2015 and Blue Point in 2017, and Calyx's Racing Post Rating of 118 puts him above both of them at the same stage.

"It was as good as it looked, it was full on," Dettori said after the comeback win. The exciting thing is there should be much more to come.

STAR RATING
★ ★ ★ ★ ★

Owner: David Armstrong
Trainer: Michael Dods

Tough speedster

MABS CROSS was a 20-1 shot when she was a two-length third to Blue Point in last year's King's Stand Stakes but she will be taken much more seriously now.

This time last year the Michael Dods-trained filly had only just started to climb up the Group-race ladder, first taking the Group 3 Palace House Stakes at Newmarket and then finishing three-quarters of a length behind Battaash when fourth in the Group 2 Temple Stakes. The King's Stand was her first step into Group 1 company but she will go back to this year's meeting as a decorated veteran of several top-level battles.

Having acquitted herself well at Royal Ascot, she went agonisingly close to Group 1 success when beaten a nose by Alpha Delphini in the Nunthorpe Stakes at York in August before she came out best in another tight finish to claim top honours by a head in the Prix de l'Abbaye *(below, red colours)* at Longchamp in October.

That completed a richly rewarding and progressive campaign as a four-year-old and, with the feeling there was still more to come, she was kept in training by owner-breeders David and Emma Armstrong.

The decision was vindicated immediately when she landed a repeat success in the Palace House on her reappearance in May, once again showing her appetite for a battle as she made light of her 9st 10lb burden, including a 7lb penalty, to get in front close home and deny Equilateral by a neck.

That earned her a career-best 117 on Racing Post Ratings (3lb above her Nunthorpe mark) and means she is rated almost a stone better than she was after her first Palace House victory. "She had to do it the hard way as she was out on a wing – that was a brilliant performance," said jockey Paul Mulrennan.

"She's a very special filly and she'll come on a lot for that too. To win the way she did with a penalty, she's the real deal."

Now she has the chance to prove she's the royal deal.

STAR RATING
★ ★ ★

Peachy Belts

www.peachybelts.co.uk
01664 454994

Beautiful Italian leather belts with detachable buckles
Handmade in England
Perfect presents for jeans wearers
See us at Cheltenham Races and Burghley Horse Trials

Moving target for champion juvenile

QUESTION marks swirled around Too Darn Hot throughout the spring but in the end the choice of big-race target was clear to trainer John Gosden and jockey Frankie Dettori.

"Do we run in the Derby or the St James's Palace? The answer is we'll freshen up and go to Royal Ascot for the St James's Palace," said

Gosden after watching Europe's champion juvenile of 2018 finish second to Telecaster on his reappearance in the Dante Stakes at York.

Dettori agreed. "He's got too much pace for the Derby – back to a mile," he said. "He was fresh, pulled very hard in the first four [furlongs] and he didn't finish. I made the ground up but the last furlong was a long way for him, bless him. He's blessed with natural speed, so we're going back to a mile."

A mile had been Too Darn Hot's initial Classic target but his reappearance was delayed by a minor setback that ruled him out of the Greenham Stakes and then the 2,000 Guineas, prompting Gosden to explore the Derby route.

Delight after Too Darn Hot's Dewhurst victory at two but he is beaten in the Dante on his comeback run at York (facing page)

Having had his answer in the Dante, Gosden is aiming for a third St James's Palace winner in six years following Kingman in 2014 and Without Parole last year. Too Darn Hot was much better than both of them as a juvenile, having won the Group 1 Dewhurst Stakes to achieve an excellent Racing Post Rating of 126, but they were strikingly progressive in the lead-up to Royal Ascot, in contrast to his troubled spring.

The Dante run was promising enough, considering Gosden had said

'Some of the question marks remain but, given a clear run through the five weeks from the Dante to the St James's Palace, Too Darn Hot has the potential to light up the first day of Ascot'

he would have preferred another week to get Too Darn Hot ready. "You're vulnerable off a layoff," he said. "He had two weeks walking, not even training."

Some of the question marks remain but, given a clear run through the five weeks from the Dante to the St James's Palace, Too Darn Hot still has the potential to light up the first day of the royal meeting.

STAR RATING
★ ★ ★ ★

137

France's first lady

GODOLPHIN hit the magic mark of 300 worldwide Group 1 wins with Castle Lady's Classic success in the Poule d'Essai des Pouliches in May and the unbeaten French filly looks set to be an important part of the team again at the royal meeting.

The Ascot battleground for Guineas fillies is the Coronation Stakes and that was the immediate thought in trainer Alex Pantall's mind after the daughter of Shamardal had scrambled home by a nose in the Pouliches.

Her margin of victory over Commes might have been tight but Castle Lady's RPR of 112 stood up well against the first three from the 1,000 Guineas at Newmarket – Hermosa earned 113 for her

win, ahead of Lady Kaya (111) and Qabala (110).

Castle Lady's battling success was all the more laudable for the fact that it came on only her third start.

She had not even made her debut when entries for the Pouliches closed in February, having been transferred from Charlie Appleby to the tranquil rural surroundings enjoyed by Pantall in the Loire Valley, but developed so rapidly that she demanded to be supplemented for the Classic at a cost of €36,000.

She started off with an all-weather win at Chantilly in March and just a month later landed the Group 3 Prix de la Grotte, a key Pouliches trial, before improving again in the Classic itself. Having swept to the front on the outside under Mickael

Barzalona, she showed admirable tenacity in a driving finish.

"She doesn't have a lot of experience and it's quite something for her to find herself in front and then fight all the way to the death," said Pantall. "She still has more physical progress to make and I think there's more to come."

In the past decade France has been represented in nine Coronations and their best representative each year has finished 251522115, which suggests Castle Lady *(below, right)* is a filly to take seriously.

STAR RATING
★★★

Sands Of Mali

Owner: Phoenix Thoroughbred & Cool Silk Partnership
Trainer: Richard Fahey

The course specialist

RICHARD FAHEY twice secured Royal Ascot success with star miler Ribchester, including the Queen Anne Stakes in 2017, and he is aiming high again with Sands Of Mali *(leading, second left)*, his latest Group 1 performer. Australia might be the end-of-season aim for The Everest, the world's richest sprint, but first up could be a serious bid for the Diamond Jubilee Stakes.

The Saturday Group 1 sprint is Fahey's only royal entry for the four-year-old, a confirmed specialist over Ascot's six furlongs after two high-class runs in elite company last season. He

was just held in the Commonwealth Cup at the royal meeting, falling half a length short of Eqtidaar, before ending the campaign with a first Group 1 success in the British Champions Sprint.

Sands Of Mali ran flat in between those two sparkling efforts and again on his seasonal debut when sixth behind Blue Point in the Al Quoz Sprint at Meydan, with Fahey saying: "I was quite disappointed with his run in Dubai, where I felt he didn't finish his race well, but it's a big ask taking on hardened pros over there."

A wet week in mid-June

might help Sands Of Mali. His Group 1 win came on soft and he has yet to win on anything faster than good, although it was good to firm when he ran so well at last year's royal meeting. "He has good form on most going but he wouldn't want it too firm," is Fahey's summary.

How much Sands Of Mali needs Ascot to be at his best is also debatable but a return to the track where he produced his RPR high of 121 should be a positive. A repeat would put him right in the shake-up again.

STAR RATING
★ ★ ★

TEN SOVEREIGNS

Aidan O'Brien won the third running of the Commonwealth Cup with Caravaggio in 2017 and is set to have another crack with Ten Sovereigns, who started 9-4 favourite for the 2,000 Guineas under Ryan Moore but was beaten almost five lengths into fifth behind stablemate Magna Grecia.

"There was always the possibility that Ten Sovereigns wouldn't quite get home," O'Brien said. "He was on the side where there was no pace and Ryan had to be more forward than he would have liked. He still ran a very good race and I would imagine we'll come back to six [furlongs] now for the Commonwealth Cup. That's the plan."

The son of No Nay Never shone over six furlongs as a juvenile, recording a Racing Post Rating of 120 for his Group 1 success in the Middle Park Stakes when he was half a length ahead of Jash, a probable Commonwealth Cup opponent.

AUXERRE

Godolphin's Lincoln winner was the archetypal 'Group horse in a handicap' at Doncaster, where he was sent off 5-2 favourite for the 19-runner mile contest and brushed his rivals aside by two and a quarter lengths.

Trainer Charlie Appleby was minded to take Auxerre's development one step at a time, possibly involving a step up in trip, although it was a sign of the four-year-old's exciting potential that he was still 14-1 third favourite for the Group 1 Queen Anne Stakes in mid-May after a somewhat inconclusive Lockinge left the mile division wide open.

BIG BROTHERS PRIDE

The three-year-old half-sister to last season's Prix Maurice de Gheest heroine Polydream has Group 1 entries in the King's Stand Stakes and Commonwealth Cup and enhanced her prospects of a cross-Channel trip with victory over 5½f in the Group 3 Prix Sigy at Chantilly in April. That was only her third start for Francois Rohaut and she was hugely impressive against some decent British yardsticks, winning by four lengths on good to soft ground. The race has proved a goldmine for finding future Group 1 sprinters and has provided a winner and a runner-up in the Commonwealth Cup in the last three years.

Six more to watch

Auxerre (left) and Khaadem (winning, above) both have Group 1 potential

KHAADEM

The Charlie Hills-trained three-year-old looks a pure sprinter, having run over six furlongs on all four starts, and he put himself in line for the Commonwealth Cup with victory in the Listed Carnarvon Stakes at Newbury on his reappearance. That mid-May contest is developing into a useful stepping stone to Friday's Group 1 sprint and Hills, who won the inaugural Commonwealth Cup in 2015 with Muhaarar, said: "I think Ascot and a stiff six will suit him. He might just prefer a little bit more give in the ground in time but he's an exciting horse."

EQUILATERAL

Charlie Hills has another up-and-coming sprinter in this four-year-old, who looks set to go for the Group 1 King's Stand Stakes. He was disappointing last season, finishing only 12th when well fancied for the Commonwealth Cup, but he has come back strongly this year and put up his best performance to date with a strong-finishing neck second to proven Group 1 sprinter Mabs Cross in the Palace House Stakes at Newmarket.

WALDGEIST

The French star would be high on Ascot's wishlist, although his participation at the royal meeting has been talked down by connections whose target in Britain is more likely to be the King George VI and Queen Elizabeth Stakes in late July. Last year's Arc fourth made a stunning return in the Prix Ganay in April, winning by four and a half lengths for a career-best 123 on Racing Post Ratings, but another clash with Arc winner Enable may have to come further down the line than the Prince of Wales's Stakes.

Barney Roy

Unexpected chance

THIS is the second coming of Godolphin's Barney Roy, who in his first incarnation as a racehorse was an impressive Royal Ascot winner for Richard Hannon in the St James's Palace Stakes two years ago. After that he was a nose second in the Eclipse and third in the International Stakes – both times behind Ulysses – to reach a peak Racing Post Rating of 124 and earn himself a place at stud.

Unfortunately his stallion career did not go well. He was found to be infertile, turning that lucrative avenue into a cul-de-sac. Late last year he was gelded and put back into training, this time with Godolphin's main trainer Charlie Appleby, and now he is on course for a return to Royal Ascot, probably in the Queen Anne Stakes or perhaps the Prince of Wales's Stakes.

Either race would put him back in the highest level of competition but Barney Roy has been comfortable in such company before and his first run for Appleby was promising enough. He made his return over the Ascot straight mile in the Listed Paradise Stakes – now

designated as a Queen Anne trial – and finished a neck second to Zaaki, who has never raced above Group 3 level but was good enough to finish third in the Hampton Court Stakes at last year's royal meeting.

Barney Roy's run was given an RPR of 116, which was pretty good after more than 18 months off the track, and Appleby was pleased. "When a horse has been off for that extended period, we need to see whether he's still got the enthusiasm and hunger and I feel he showed us all the right signs at Ascot," he said. "He got into a battle and didn't shirk out of it and he's entitled to come forward from that run."

It would be quite some story if his next run brought more Royal Ascot glory.

STAR RATING

★★★

Dee Ex Bee

Owner: Sheikh Hamdan Bin Mohammed Al Maktoum
Trainer: Mark Johnston

Beeline for the bonus

MARK JOHNSTON knows what it takes to win the Gold Cup, having done so three times in eight years with Double Trigger and Royal Rebel in a halcyon period with his stayers, and he reckons Dee Ex Bee is made of the right stuff.

The 2019 Gold Cup is shaping up as a red-hot contest, with defending champion Stradivarius and Melbourne Cup winner Cross Counter heading the ante-post betting, but Dee Ex Bee put himself in the reckoning with a clear-cut victory in the Group 3 Sagaro Stakes at Ascot on his seasonal debut in May.

The Sagaro over 2m has long been a key prep for the 2m4f Gold Cup and, just as significantly nowadays, it is one of the eight starting points for the Weatherbys Hamilton Stayers' Million – the £1m bonus if a horse wins one of those races and goes on to take the Gold Cup, the Goodwood Cup in July and the Lonsdale Cup at York in August.

Stradivarius pulled off the hugely valuable four-timer last year and the bonus was certainly in Johnston's mind when he targeted the Sagaro with Dee Ex Bee, who passed the first test with flying colours when he came home three and a quarter lengths clear under William Buick.

Double Trigger might easily have landed the bonus if it had been around in 1995 – when he won the Sagaro, Henry II Stakes, Gold Cup, Goodwood Cup and Doncaster Cup – and Johnston has taken up the gauntlet. "It takes an awful lot of winning but that's why we came here [to the Sagaro] first," he said.

Dee Ex Bee's Sagaro win was his best performance on Racing Post Ratings since he was second to Masar in last year's Derby, with his form having tailed off somewhat in the second half of last season even though he was still fourth in the St Leger, and Buick was impressed. "He certainly feels as if he'll be a horse for the Gold Cup," he said. "He felt like a horse who will get the trip as well as any of them. He's got that bit of class too."

The four-year-old will have to step up again, having been beaten four and a half lengths into second by Cross Counter in the Gordon Stakes at Goodwood last August, but Johnston believes he is classy enough to make his mark.

"The staying division has got tougher and tougher. You need a proper Group 1 horse, ideally one who was a Classic horse at three, and that's what this horse was," said Johnston, whose last Gold Cup victory was in 2002 when Royal Rebel completed back-to-back successes.

"You can't put him up there with Royal Rebel and Double Trigger yet, but thankfully I've got a St Leger horse staying in training to go for the Gold Cup – and that's what I've been dreaming of over the last ten years."

STAR RATING

★★★

Guineas winner must

MAGNA GRECIA became the tenth 2,000 Guineas winner for Aidan O'Brien with his two-and-a-half-length success at Newmarket in May and he will become the fourth to double up in the St James's Palace Stakes if he is successful in that Royal Ascot mission.

Not all of the previous nine have tried but Ascot's short straight presents a different challenge to the wide expanse of Newmarket and being able to win on both tracks is the mark of a superior miler.

The jury remains out on Magna Grecia in that regard, principally owing to doubts over the standard of the Newmarket field – in the absence of 2018 champion juvenile Too Darn Hot – and the value of the form on the day. Undoubtedly he benefited from being part of the trio that raced on the stands' side – along with 66-1 runner-up King Of Change and sixth-placed Shine So Bright – and his winning RPR of 121 was the joint-lowest of the past decade.

Donnacha O'Brien's mount won comprehensively, however, and he would have come out as the best horse in the race even if the centre group was rated 3-4lb better than the bare form.

now pass different test

Magna Grecia followed a classic route to Classic success, having won the Group 1 Vertem Futurity on his final start at two, and his overall form lines read well. His only defeat as a juvenile came in the Group 3 Autumn Stakes when he went down by a neck to French raider Persian King, who scored his own Classic success in the Poule d'Essai des Poulains the week after Magna Grecia's Guineas victory.

Winning the Futurity over a mile as a juvenile can be the precursor to a middle-distance campaign as the next season unfolds but the thinking was different with Magna Grecia, as O'Brien explained at Newmarket. "John Magnier always thought he'd be a miler, and he knows pedigrees like no-one else. He's a lovely horse who has developed a lot of speed. He's very exciting."

What is also exciting is that Too Darn Hot – the absent champion at Newmarket – could well be lying in wait in the St James's Palace Stakes. It's a showdown that should answer a lot of questions.

STAR RATING

★★★★

145

Owner: Sheikh Mohammed Bin Khalifa Al Thani
Trainer: Roger Varian

Potential Ascot queen

THE Newmarket Guineas races both threw up some measure of hard luck, suggesting the form might be turned around in later rematches, and 1,000 Guineas third Qabala certainly looks to have strong claims in the Coronation Stakes if she gets a smoother run up Ascot's short straight than she had at Newmarket.

The Roger Varian-trained filly finished a length and a quarter behind Hermosa in the Guineas and, while it would be a stretch to say she would have won but for David Egan briefly having difficulty finding a run, it didn't help that she ended up challenging on the far side from a rather exposed position.

"She was a little short of room at the top of the hill," said Varian. "David thought it cost him a length because he couldn't hold his pitch and had to come around Fairyland. I was a bit disappointed not to win but I thought Qabala ran great. She looks a Group 1 filly."

The Coronation is an obvious Group 1 for the diary and there is considerable cause for optimism with Qabala, whose Guineas run was only the third of her career. She won a 7f fillies' maiden at Newmarket on her sole start as a juvenile and jumped to Guineas favouritism after

taking the Group 3 Nell Gwyn Stakes on her reappearance in April.

The rest of the first six in the Guineas all had considerably more experience and had run in a Group 1 before, marking out Qabala as potentially the biggest improver.

Five of the last eight Coronation winners to have run at Newmarket had suffered Guineas defeat and, with Group 1 experience now under her belt, Qabala could be another who does better at the royal meeting.

STAR RATING
★★★★

King Of Change

Owner: Ali Abdulla Saeed
Trainer: Richard Hannon

Surprise package

LAST year Tip Two Win ran a cracker to finish second in the 2,000 Guineas at 50-1 but failed to build on that promise when fourth in the St James's Palace Stakes next time before sinking back into obscurity.

Twelve months on we have another big-priced Guineas runner-up in 66-1 shot King Of Change *(below)* and he, too, is likely to head for the St James's Palace. Why should the story be any different this time?

One reason why it might not is that there appeared to be a bias towards those drawn high in the Guineas and King Of Change was one of the main beneficiaries. Most of the 19 runners raced up the centre, while only three stuck to the stands' side, but the advantage lay with the smaller group – winner Magna Grecia, King Of Change and sixth-placed Shine So Bright, a 16-1 shot.

Yet there is no denying that King Of Change is much improved as a three-year-old. He ran in two lowly contests at Nottingham and Wolverhampton as a juvenile, finishing second both times, but was marked out by Hannon as one to note before his reappearance win, again at Nottingham in a 1m½f novice.

"He progressed well physically over the winter and won well at Nottingham," the trainer said after the Guineas, before addressing the subject of the Newmarket draw: "I know the others were stuck out in the middle but he's still run a huge race."

Was it a fluke? Only time will tell.

STAR RATING
★★★

Army on the march

"IF the ground isn't too quick at Ascot, he should have a favourite's chance." That was quite a statement by James Tate as he set his sights on a first Group 1 success with Invincible Army in the Diamond Jubilee Stakes, but the positive tone reflected the trainer's new-found confidence in his rising star.

Invincible Army had shown flashes of top-flight potential with a Group 3 victory and second place in the Group 2 Sandy Lane Stakes on his first two starts of 2018 – both against subsequent Group 1 winners – but he wasn't quite ready for the highest level and could finish only ninth in the Commonwealth Cup at Royal Ascot.

He has made rapid strides as a four-year-old, advancing his career-best Racing Post Rating to 116 with a Listed victory at Doncaster on his reappearance and again to 119 when he took the Group 2 Duke of York Stakes by two and a quarter lengths from Major Jumbo.

"He seems to be different this year, he's calm and just has the mentality for it," said Tate after that first Group 2 victory of his burgeoning career. "We have to think of the Group 1s only and he appears to get the six furlongs well, so we've got Ascot, the Haydock Sprint Cup and the Champions Sprint and they'll be the three targets."

Being a late developer runs in Invincible Army's family. His sire Invincible Spirit landed his Group 1 in the Haydock Sprint Cup as a five-year-old and his dam Rajeem reached the same high in the Falmouth Stakes on the tenth and final start of her two-season career.

His parents won their Group 1s on good to firm ground and Invincible Army coped with those fast conditions in the Duke of York but, as Tate suggested, a dry week at Ascot could be a concern. Invincible Army's better form had been on good or slower prior to the York win and he was twice well beaten on good to firm last season.

"I was a little concerned about the ground [at York] but as long as it's safe he's okay," is Tate's view. As long as conditions do not compromise him, Invincible Army looks more than okay.

STAR RATING
★ ★ ★ ★

'He has made rapid strides as a four-year-old, advancing his career-best Racing Post Rating to 116 with a Listed victory at Doncaster and again to 119 when he took the Group 2 Duke of York Stakes from Major Jumbo'

Derby hero on comeback trail

A DERBY winner running at Royal Ascot the following year is a rare event and hosting Masar's return from injury would be quite a coup for the track. A comeback victory would be even more special.

The last Derby winner to turn up at the royal meeting the following season was Camelot in 2013, and prior to him it was Sir Percy in 2007. Before them, you have to go back not years but decades. The last horse to win at Royal Ascot after landing the Derby was Royal Palace in the 1968 Prince of Wales's Stakes.

The same race is a possible target for Masar as trainer Charlie Appleby plots a route back from the injury that has kept the first Derby winner in Godolphin blue on the sidelines since his Epsom triumph.

"We've made the entries for Royal Ascot in the Prince of Wales's and the Hardwicke," Appleby said. "It's a day-by-day situation but he helps himself in potentially getting to Ascot as he's an athlete and a very clean-winded horse."

On the subject of going for the 1m2f Prince of Wales's, rather than the Hardwicke Stakes over the Derby trip of 1m4f, the trainer added: "William [Buick] and I spoke about it and we feel the mile and a quarter will be the right starting point for

'At this stage it would be a victory to get him back on track. If that's at Royal Ascot, that would be a win-win'

him. It's a trip we've not explored, but potentially he shows it to be the right spot to start him off."

Masar has high-class form at a mile, having finished third to Saxon Warrior in last year's 2,000 Guineas, but he stepped straight up to 1m4f for his next start in the Derby and has not raced again since. In both Classics he finished ahead of Roaring Lion, who carried on

improving to win four Group 1 races over 1m to 1m2f, and the hope is that Masar can make similar progress as a four-year-old given Appleby's careful handling of his recuperation.

At this stage it would be a victory to get him back on track. If that's at Royal Ascot, that would be a win-win.

STAR RATING
★ ★ ★ ★

Skardu

Scarred but ready to fight

SKARDU did not have the luck of the draw when he was third in the 2,000 Guineas, but that run at least showed he belonged in Group 1 company and trainer William Haggas's immediate thought was to give him another shot at top-level success in the St James's Palace Stakes.

The opening-day Group 1 is a traditional meeting place for the settling of old scores and the establishment of new rivalries as the Guineas form from Britain, Ireland and France is put to the test. Skardu looks likely to have a say, having put himself in the debate by coming out best in the 'wrong' group at Newmarket.

The centre of the track turned out to be a disadvantage for the 16 runners who raced there, led home by Skardu, with the first two places going to Magna Grecia and King Of Change from the trio who raced on the stands' side.

Many would take the view that Magna Grecia was the best horse on the day anyway, given that he was two and a half lengths clear of King Of Change and just over four ahead of Skardu. He will continue to be a formidable rival as the season unfolds but Haggas would hope for a closer contest on fairer terms.

"He's run a great race but it's a shame there was a draw advantage – there clearly was one," the trainer said after Skardu's Guineas run. "I feared the worst when the stalls opened, although the winner has bolted up and would have won wherever he was drawn."

At that stage Skardu was also behind Magna Grecia in terms of experience. Whereas the Guineas winner had scored at Group 1 level as a juvenile, Skardu had nothing more than a 7f Newmarket maiden win in his first season. He was reported to have wintered well before winning the Group 3 Craven Stakes *(below)* on his reappearance to set up his Guineas tilt.

Haggas's son of Shamardal is open to further improvement and it is interesting to note that since 2000 eight beaten horses from the Newmarket Guineas have won the St James's Palace, compared with only six winners who followed up at Royal Ascot.

A battle may have been lost but the war is still there to be won.

STAR RATING
★★★

Magical

Owner: Derrick Smith, Mrs John Magnier & Michael Tabor
Trainer Aidan O'Brien

Strong form lines

MAGICAL was beaten in five Group 1 races before she finally won one – at Ascot of all places – but her subsequent record suggests there will be more success to come in 2019. With form that ties in with the top fillies around, she would be a serious contender if she turns up at the royal meeting.

That top-level breakthrough came in the British Champions Fillies & Mares Stakes last October on only her second start at 1m4f, having stepped up from a mile. It had been a long time coming, mainly because of an injury-hit season in 2018 that forced trainer Aidan O'Brien to give up on Classics plans and hold her back for the autumn.

Having raised her game to beat Group 1 performers Coronet (previously second to Sea Of Class) and Lah Ti Dar at Ascot, Magical took her form to another level in defeat when she ran dual Prix de l'Arc de Triomphe winner Enable to three-quarters of a length in the Breeders' Cup Turf. Only four weeks before, on her first try at 1m4f in the Arc, Magical had been a well-beaten tenth behind Enable as a 40-1 shot.

Even if it could be argued that Enable was a little below her best in America, it was still an impressive effort by Magical to get so close and finish nine lengths clear of the third-placed horse. "Everything went perfectly to plan and Magical has been beaten by a great filly," O'Brien said at the Breeders' Cup.

A couple of weeks earlier, after the Ascot victory, he had reflected on Magical's journey. "We thought she was going to be a serious contender for the Oaks at Epsom but she got an injury ten days before the race. She was then still only just coming back in the Arc. Wayne Lordan was brilliant that day as he said there's no doubt this filly gets a mile and a half."

What has never been in doubt is Magical's pedigree for the highest level. She is by supersire Galileo out of Halfway To Heaven, a three-time Group 1 winner over 1m-1m2f, which makes her a sister to another triple Group 1 winner in Rhododendron.

Having kept Magical in training as a four-year-old, her connections will be expecting big things.

STAR RATING

★★★★

TOP HORSES

KEW GARDENS
ASCOT FORM: 1

Having come up short on the Derby route last year, Kew Gardens started on a different Classic trail with victory in the Queen's Vase at the royal meeting. That ultimately led to St Leger success and marked him out as a potential Gold Cup challenger for Aidan O'Brien, although he started slowly again this season when he was only second at odds-on in the Ormonde at Chester (a qualifying race for the £1m stayers' bonus). Estimate, Leading Light and Stradivarius have all done the Queen's Vase/Gold Cup double since 2013.

ACCIDENTAL AGENT
ASCOT FORM: 71431

Last year's 33-1 Queen Anne Stakes winner heads back there off an encouraging third on his reappearance in the Lockinge Stakes, which marked an improvement on sixth in the Newbury race 12 months earlier and certainly on his disappointing form since his Royal Ascot triumph. "It's great to have him back as we had a lot of doubters," said trainer Eve Johnson Houghton after the Lockinge. "All roads lead to the Queen Anne. We know he loves Ascot and this will bring him on in leaps and bounds."

SOLDIER'S CALL
ASCOT FORM: 1

Fast-rising Lambourn trainer Archie Watson found his flagbearer last year with Soldier's Call, who gave him a first Royal Ascot success in the Windsor Castle Stakes, a first Group 3, a first Group 2 and very nearly a first Group 1 when beaten a neck into third in the Prix de l'Abbaye. Watson has set his sights on the top level again, aiming for the King's Stand Stakes, and Soldier's Call started off well enough with a Listed third under a penalty at York on his reappearance.

RIPP ORF
ASCOT FORM: 13125

The David Elsworth-trained five-year-old missed the royal meeting last year but compiled an excellent record

Six Ascot form horses

Ripp Orf (main picture) and Aidan O'Brien's Kew Gardens have won at Ascot

at the track in 7f big-field handicaps. He won the 27-runner Victoria Cup, finished third in the International (27 runners), won the Cunard Handicap (20 runners) and was second in the Challenge Cup (15 runners). Fifth in the Victoria Cup this year, he still looks attractive off a mark of 94 (1lb higher than his Cunard win).

BAGHDAD
ASCOT FORM: 1

Last year's King George V Handicap winner has come back even better this year and his 1m4f handicap win at Newmarket's Guineas meeting had trainer Mark Johnston thinking about the Duke of Edinburgh Handicap this year, although he also has an ambitious entry, for a colt rated 104, in the Group 2 Hardwicke Stakes. Johnston has won the Duke of Edinburgh three times with similar four-year-olds who were all double-figure prices.

LORD GLITTERS
ASCOT FORM: 21226

David O'Meara's six-year-old was highly progressive before his disappointing 13th in the Group 1 Lockinge Stakes but don't rule out a return to form in the Queen Anne Stakes. He was runner-up at 20-1 last year behind Accidental Agent, having followed that rival up from handicaps – they had also been first and second in the Challenge Cup at Ascot in the autumn of 2017 before Lord Glitters landed the Balmoral Handicap on British Champions Day.

Owner: Godolphin
Trainer: Charlie Appleby

Primed for big summer

GODOLPHIN and Charlie Appleby made big news with Masar and Cross Counter in a tremendous 2018 and there are high hopes that Old Persian could be another headline-maker for the resurgent team.

The son of Dubawi achieved a considerable amount as a three-year-old last season, winning the King Edward VII Stakes at Royal Ascot and a strong Great Voltigeur Stakes at York, but the signs pointed to bigger and better after an impressive winter campaign in Dubai.

Old Persian landed a first Group 1 triumph in the Dubai Sheema Classic over 1m4f, showing an impressive turn of foot to improve his Racing Post Rating to 122, and Appleby is confident he belongs in the best company.

"He's a class animal, a typical Dubawi colt who has made that great progression," he said. "We may drop to 1m2f for the Prince of Wales's Stakes, working back from the King George, which is the kind of race he

deserves to be going for."

The Group 2 Hardwicke over 1m4f is the other possible target at Royal Ascot, if the shorter trip of the Group 1 Prince of Wales's is deemed too much of a test at this stage, but either way Old Persian's tactical and finishing speed will make him a dangerous opponent.

Like Appleby, jockey William Buick was impressed after the Sheema Classic. "I have to give credit to the horse," he said. "He finds his own passage and from three to four he's really improved and he has a big turn of foot now. It was a beautiful performance."

Old Persian's form had substance last year, when he beat subsequent Irish Derby runner-up Rostropovich at Royal Ascot and got the better of Cross Counter and Kew Gardens in the Great Voltigeur, and it is getting better all the time.

STAR RATING
★★★★

Jubiloso

Bred for Ascot stardom

REGALLY bred three-year-old Jubiloso has made rapid strides towards a Royal Ascot assignment, which will come less than two months after her first racecourse appearance.

That debut came on the all-weather at Chelmsford on a Thursday night in late April, a world away from the glamour of the royal meeting. She made easy work of her task, scoring by just under three lengths over 6f, and three weeks later Sir Michael Stoute sent her for a 7f novice on turf at Newbury.

This time she was even more dominant with a highly impressive seven-length victory over 11 outclassed rivals, prompting single-figure quotes for the Group 1 Coronation Stakes, and connections did not hide their excitement.

Ted Durcan, the former Classic-winning jockey, was representing Stoute. "She's a filly Sir Michael and anyone who has had anything to do with her have always held in the highest esteem," he said.

"She's got an amazing attitude and a temperament to die for. She's got a smashing pedigree and she's done nothing but please everyone who has been around her."

Teddy Grimthorpe, owner Khalid Abdullah's racing manager, said: "We don't have a definite plan, but I'd hope Sir Michael would want to head to Royal Ascot, but what guise that might take is hard to tell. I suppose she could do the Sandringham, Jersey or Coronation Stakes."

As for her rapid progress, he added: "She didn't surprise us [at Newbury] and we've always liked her. She's shown a good deal of ability at home, but that doesn't always translate to the racecourse. When Jubiloso won at Chelmsford she was a bit green. One minute she was fourth being pushed along and then suddenly, and almost deceptively, she came through. It could have been a bit of greenness, but she won well and her work since had been encouraging. From that point of view we were pretty hopeful but the style she did it in [at Newbury] was visually impressive. She's got a fantastic pedigree."

Jubiloso is certainly bred for the royal meeting. Her sire Shamardal was a St James's Palace Stakes winner and her dam Joyeuse is a half-sister to the great Frankel, twice a Royal Ascot winner in his glittering career.

STAR RATING
★★★★

TOP HORSES

THE TIN MAN
ASCOT FORM: 14811547

James Fanshawe's hardy sprinter is seven now and still capable of high-class form, as he showed with victory in the Group 1 Haydock Sprint Cup last September. He can never be discounted at Ascot, his favourite track. He has won three of his eight starts there, including his other two Group 1 successes in the 2016 British Champions Sprint and 2017 Diamond Jubilee Stakes, and twice been fourth in Group 1s. His Haydock win (the best of his career on RPR) was on heavy ground but usually the faster conditions at Royal Ascot suit him well.

THOMAS HOBSON
ASCOT FORM: 1262

The tough stayer was a hurdler for two seasons before Willie Mullins sent him to Royal Ascot in 2017 to win the Ascot Handicap and finish runner-up in the Queen Alexandra Stakes four days later. He was sixth in the Queen Alexandra last year before ending his season with second behind Stradivarius in the Long Distance Cup on Ascot's Champions Day. The nine-year-old was beaten at odds-on in the Oleander-Rennen (a qualifying race for the £1m stayers' bonus) in Germany on his reappearance, which could mean he goes for the Queen Alexandra again rather than the Gold Cup.

MAJOR JUMBO
ASCOT FORM: 33

Kevin Ryan's sprinter has stepped out of handicaps into Group races since his pair of Ascot thirds last summer in the 6f Wokingham and the 5f Bet

Six more Ascot form horses

Ascot aces: (clockwise from main picture) high fives after Signora Cabello's Queen Mary victory; The Tin Man; Le Brivido; Bless Him

BLESS HIM
ASCOT FORM: 197

The 2017 Britannia winner had niggling problems last year that prevented him from hitting the heights again, although he was not disgraced when ninth in the Royal Hunt Cup (third in the far-side group). Trainer David Simcock kept the son of Sea The Stars for 31,000gns when Qatar Racing sent him to the sales last autumn. Gelded over the winter, Bless Him shaped promisingly for another Hunt Cup tilt on his return in the Hambleton at York in May.

SIGNORA CABELLO
ASCOT FORM: 14

John Quinn's three-year-old filly is on track to bid for the Queen Mary/King's Stand double achieved by American flyer Lady Aurelia in 2016-17. She was fourth to Calyx over 6f in the Commonwealth Cup trial on her reappearance but will be better suited by a drop in trip given her form over 5-5½f (four straight wins after a debut fourth) as well as her liking for the track. She won the Queen Mary at 25-1 and could get involved at big odds again.

With Ascot Heritage Handicap, but that big-field track experience could help him make a mark at big odds if he goes for the King's Stand Stakes. His Group form is good against the likes of Mabs Cross (last year's King's Stand third).

LE BRIVIDO
ASCOT FORM: 1

Le Brivido was flying at the finish when fifth in the Lockinge Stakes on his second start for Aidan O'Brien, setting him up well

for an expected crack at the Queen Anne Stakes. Trained by Andre Fabre until this season, the five-year-old looked set for top honours two seasons ago when he followed second place in the French 2,000 Guineas with victory in the Jersey Stakes at Royal Ascot but he was plagued by injury and raced only once more for Fabre. Albeit with an extra year in between, he will be trying for the Jersey/Queen Anne double achieved recently by Ribchester.

Group 1 ambitions

A FIRST Group 1 victory is the target for Crystal Ocean this season and that may well steer connections towards the rarefied atmosphere of the Prince of Wales's Stakes rather than the easier pickings of a repeat win in the Group 2 Hardwicke Stakes.

Once again the high-class and consistent five-year-old has shown success at the top level should not be beyond him with a pair of relatively stress-free victories in the same Group 3 contests he took en route to last year's royal meeting. First he won the 1m2f Gordon Richards Stakes at Sandown a little more easily than last year and then he landed the 1m4f Al Rayyan Stakes at Newbury a little less easily but still comfortably enough by two lengths.

That would give him strong claims again in the Hardwicke but after the Newbury victory Sir Michael Stoute was eyeing the more ambitious route. "My preference at this stage would be the Prince of Wales's Stakes. He's very versatile trip-wise. He did it well at Sandown over ten furlongs," he said.

Crystal Ocean has had three previous attempts at Group 1 level and finished second each time, twice going close with a half-length defeat by Capri in the 2017 St Leger and last year's neck margin behind stablemate Poet's Word in the King George and Queen Elizabeth Stakes.

A mile and a half is unquestionably Crystal Ocean's best distance and he reached a career high of 127 on Racing Post Ratings in the King George, which he repeated next time when runner-up behind the reappearing Enable in the

Group 3 September Stakes at Kempton. He could meet Enable again in the Prince of Wales's and would do so on 5lb better terms for a three-and-a-half-length defeat.

His best RPR over 1m2f is 123 in this year's Gordon Richards and his only Group 1 participation over that trip, in last year's Champion Stakes, resulted in a heavy loss by six lengths behind Cracksman, which may be taken as an indication of the scale of the task awaiting him in the Prince of Wales's.

What's certain is that Crystal Ocean will give it his best shot.

STAR RATING
★ ★ ★ ★

Southern France

Owner: Derrick Smith, Mrs John Magnier & Michael Tabor; Trainer: Aidan O'Brien

Stayer picks up pace

SOUTHERN FRANCE has been a nearly horse for the past 12 months, performing to a consistent level but often having to play second fiddle to a stablemate, but there is a sense that perseverance may soon be rewarded.

That was reflected in a positive message from Aidan O'Brien as he laid out plans for Royal Ascot. The expectation was that Southern France, who had just finished second to Stradivarius in the Yorkshire Cup, was being prepared for the Gold Cup but the trainer said the Hardwicke Stakes over a mile shorter was under consideration too.

"We haven't yet made a plan for Southern France but it's quite possible we might aim for the Hardwicke rather than the Gold Cup," O'Brien said. "He ran a very good race at York and showed more pace then we thought he had."

Southern France did not make his debut until late April last year as a three-year-old but progressed quickly to land a 1m4f maiden on his second start and a 1m5f Listed race on his third.

He stepped up again for the Group 2 Queen's Vase over 1m6f at Royal Ascot but was a well-beaten second behind stablemate Kew

Close contest: Southern France (right) battles it out with Stradivarius

Gardens, who went on to land the St Leger with Southern France again well behind in third.

In between, Southern France was fourth in a Group 3 at the Curragh, beaten by two stablemates, and after the St Leger he was sent off 4-1 favourite for the Cesarewitch at Newmarket but came home in seventh.

He started with another Group 3 defeat on his reappearance but then gave

Stradivarius a fright in the 1m6f Yorkshire Cup, going down by three-quarters of a length after a hard-fought battle.

O'Brien has other options for the Gold Cup and now, given his assessment of the Yorkshire Cup run, with Southern France too. It will be interesting to see which way he goes.

STAR RATING

★ ★ ★

TOP HORSES

KYNREN

'Deserving' to win a big handicap is a rather strange concept but the David Barron-trained five-year-old has certainly been knocking hard on the door. He was only 21st in last year's Royal Hunt Cup but last season he went on to finish third in the John Smith's Cup at York and a neck second in another valuable York handicap, and this season he has been runner-up to 'good thing' Auxerre in the Lincoln and a neck second to Cape Byron in the 7f Victoria Cup at Ascot. He likes easy ground but goes well on fast and is a leading Hunt Cup contender.

SPACE BLUES

Charlie Appleby has a prime candidate for the Britannia in the progressive Space Blues, who stepped into handicap company for the first time at York in May and scored by two lengths in a 19-runner field off a mark of 93. That was only his fourth run and, with his sharp turn of foot and big-field experience, he looks capable of further improvement.

CORGI

Hughie Morrison is a shrewd operator in the Royal Ascot handicaps and Corgi looks well set up for a tilt at the 1m4f Duke of Edinburgh (which the trainer has won three times already) after his reappearance third over that trip in the competitive Jorvik Handicap at York in mid-May. The form looks solid as the winner was First Eleven, a close third when Corgi was runner-up in last year's King George V Handicap at the royal meeting.

EMBOUR

Having struggled in big handicaps last year, Embour has come of age as a four-year-old and put himself in the Wokingham picture with 6f wins on the Kempton all-weather and at Newbury. "He's a smashing horse now and will be a nice horse in big handicaps," said trainer Richard Hannon after the Newbury win. "I wasn't sure dropping him in was the right thing to do – because last time it looked like the trip was insufficient – but clearly it was. He's on the way up. He'll love the stiff finish at Ascot."

PERSIAN MOON

Mark Johnston likes to target the middle-distance/staying races and one of his possibles is Persian Moon, who did reasonably well in a couple of Classic trials (notably when a

Solid form: Corgi (main picture) and Kynren (right, above)

Six handicappers to watch

close third to Bangkok at Sandown). He is entered in the Group 2 King Edward VII Stakes but could also come under consideration for the King George V Handicap off a mark of 101. He is battle-hardened after seven runs as a juvenile and that experience could be put to good use at Royal Ascot.

CHELKAR

Willie Mullins is likely to have a big team for the Ascot Handicap again and last year's fourth Chelkar could slip under the radar. The six-year-old ran an eye-catching race on his first start for the stable behind Lagostovegas on fast ground last year and was perhaps

unsuited by the way the race unfolded. He lost form afterwards but his later runs were over shorter trips on slower ground and

Mullins could freshen him up to peak for the big day off a 2lb higher mark.

Mustashry

Owner: Hamdan Al Maktoum
Trainer: Sir Michael Stoute

Late developer takes the lead

IN A mile division crying out for a leader of the pack, Mustashry came to the fore with a comprehensive two-and-a-half-length victory over a host of fellow wannabes in the Lockinge Stakes at Newbury in May.

Whether that advantage will hold when it comes to the Queen Anne Stakes is open to some question. The royal meeting's curtain-raiser proved below par last year, when Accidental Agent caused a 33-1 upset, and there appear to be holes in the form again.

On the positive side Mustashry's Lockinge victory was solid enough, worth 122 on Racing Post Ratings, and his improvement into a proper Group 1 performer at the age of six might well be genuine given that he is trained by Sir Michael Stoute, a past master with older horses.

That was the view of Lockinge-winning jockey Jim Crowley, who said: "He feels different this year and the way he put the race to bed was very good. We thought he was up to it and he's trained by a genius. Sir Michael is a great trainer and every year he brings horses on."

Stoute suggested a clean bill of health had made the difference and paid tribute to the efforts of groom Jade Ransley behind the scenes. "Jade has made this horse," he said. "She looks after him like no other could and puts a lot of work into him. He's had a lot of niggles over his career but I don't think we've ever had him in better form."

On the other hand Mustashry had looked a solid Group 2 performer rather than a Group 1 star in waiting before the Lockinge and a crucial factor may have been that he had the advantage of a previous run this season over the placed horses, Laurens and Accidental Agent.

That suggests the Queen Anne could be a closer affair and Mustashry will have to prove himself all over again.

STAR RATING
★ ★ ★

Mustashry leads home Laurens in the Lockinge at Newbury

Laurens

Owner: John Dance
Trainer: Karl Burke

Classy filly up for the fight

LAURENS lost the first battle in the mile division, going down by two and a half lengths to Mustashry in the Group 1 Lockinge Stakes at Newbury, but her connections are confident the war can be won.

"She's going to be a force in this division," said trainer Karl Burke after the Lockinge. "She'll come on a length or two and the Queen Anne is the plan."

The royal meeting's curtain-raiser is the next battleground in a wide-open mile division and Burke will not be the only trainer fancying a turnaround in the Lockinge form. The first five, and possibly more, could all cross swords again down the Ascot straight mile.

Burke, though, has more reason than most to be confident of his challenger's ability to make her mark at the top level. Laurens was a four-time Group 1 winner last year – and once as a two-year-old – and the only unproven aspect of that record is whether she can beat male rivals.

Last year's Group 1 successes came against fillies, albeit some of them from the older generation, in the Prix Saint-Alary, Prix de Diane, Matron Stakes and Sun Chariot Stakes. What they proved above all was Laurens' fighting spirit, as she won by no more than three-quarters of a length on ground ranging from good to firm to good to soft.

"The mile division probably lacks a real superstar and hopefully she's there to fill that gap," Burke said. "She's a high-class horse. She has proved that each year she has run. We think she has improved again. She has certainly improved physically and as she has got stronger she has probably got quicker."

Burke conceded before her reappearance that "her first two races against the colts could be her hardest of the year, as the other races, if we stick at a mile, are probably going to be against fillies".

The second of those tests now awaits her in the Queen Anne.

STAR RATING
★ ★ ★ ★

'Laurens was a four-time Group 1 winner last year – and once as a two-year-old'

City Light

Owner: Ecurie JL Bouchard/Madame I Corbani
Trainer: Stephane Wattel

Unlucky loser

FOR a fleeting moment following last year's Diamond Jubilee Stakes, Stephane Wattel thought City Light had provided him with a breakthrough Group 1 win after three decades as a trainer. But the judge's call revealed Merchant Navy had denied the French raider by a short head and Wattel's long wait went on.

Connections were left to rue a cruel finish where City Light appeared to be in front a stride after the line and what might have been had their livewire sprinter not reared in the stalls moments before the start – "I don't think it helped, that's for

sure," said joint-owner John Corbani.

City Light never got as close again in two more Group 1 attempts last year but Wattel is likely to send the five-year-old back across the Channel for another crack at the Diamond Jubilee.

That would make sense as City Light has produced his best two performances in Britain, recording a Racing Post Rating of 116 in winning the All-Weather Sprint Championships at Lingfield last March before

stepping up to an RPR of 121 in the Diamond Jubilee.

Clearly he is suited by the all-weather and fast ground on Ascot's sand-based track, so much so that his RPR at the royal meeting ranked him among the top half-dozen European sprinters of last year.

He has a serious opponent on home turf in Godolphin's Inns Of Court, who won by half a length when they clashed in a Listed 6f contest at Maisons-Laffitte in April on their seasonal debuts, and they could bring that rivalry to Royal Ascot.

STAR RATING
★★★

Ghaiyyath

Owner: Godolphin
Trainer: Charlie Appleby

Powerhouse galloper

THE Prix de l'Arc de Triomphe is the long-term target for Ghaiyyath and a step up to 1m4f does not look too far away. Perhaps that first attempt over the Arc trip could come at Royal Ascot.

That possibility increased with the four-year-old's odds-on defeat in the Group 1 Prix Ganay over 1m2½f at Longchamp in late April. Ghaiyyath was coming off a Group 2 win at the same track but found Waldgeist and Study Of Man too hot to handle, drawing an honest assessment from trainer Charlie Appleby.

"We knew coming into the race it would be a test for him," he said. "Group 1 horses generally have a gear change. That's why they are

what they are. They sat close to him, he was there to be picked up and that's what happened."

Where does that leave Ghaiyyath? For a start it left him still around the 10-1 mark in the ante-post betting for the Prince of Wales's Stakes. That demonstrated high regard for a colt who has yet to win above Group 2 level but might have been a Classics player last year if he had not been forced to miss most of the campaign through injury.

On the other hand, the Prince of Wales's is shaping up as an even hotter Group 1 test over 1m2f and there would have to be serious doubt over whether Ghaiyyath would cope any better than in the Ganay.

Appleby's stated preference after the Ganay was to step him up to 1m4f and that would bring the Group 2 Hardwicke Stakes into play. It is a race ideally suited to Ghaiyyath's talents, as described by his trainer. "I wouldn't say he lacks a change of gear, but he's a big, powerful horse and his biggest asset is that when he gets to the front he's relentless and just keeps piling it on."

After his long absence last year, and with the Ganay being only his sixth outing, Ghaiyyath remains capable of piling on more improvement.

STAR RATING
★★★

TOP HORSES

MAGNETIC CHARM

A winner for the Queen at Royal Ascot is something special and there will be huge interest in this three-year-old as the meeting draws near. The William Haggas-trained filly put herself in the picture with a neck victory in Listed company on her reappearance at York's May meeting, having shown promise in four starts as a juvenile.

She was being aimed at the Sandringham Handicap but was already close to the ceiling rating of 105 before her York victory and that could mean she is thrown into Group 1 company in the Coronation Stakes.

Haggas's wife Maureen said: "We brought her [to York] to tee her up for Ascot and we know she'll improve for the run, so that was encouraging. We were looking at the Sandringham but she's in the Coronation as well and after what she has done, we might have to raise our thinking towards that race."

ENTITLE

This John Gosden-trained three-year-old could join her illustrious half-sister Enable on the stable's team for the royal meeting. She is not in Enable's class but took a big step forward to dead-heat for second in the Group 3 Musidora Stakes at York's May meeting on only her third start, setting up another step up in class and distance to contest the Group 2 Ribblesdale Stakes over 1m4f. "Entitle was very green and was on and off the bridle [at York]. She'll have learned a lot. We'll probably take her to the Ribblesdale," said Gosden, who won that contest most recently with Coronet in 2017.

Fairyland: sprint option for 1,000 Guineas fifth

Six fillies to watch

AGROTERA

The Ed Walker-trained four-year-old has already achieved Royal Ascot success, having landed last year's Sandringham Handicap in decisive style, but may need some help from officialdom to do so again in the Group 2 Duke of Cambridge Stakes.

Agrotera took another step up the ladder with a Listed victory on her reappearance in the Snowdrop Fillies' Stakes at Kempton, where she was allowed to be accompanied by former racehorse Dannios in the preliminaries. "Fair play to the stewards for allowing Dannios into the paddock, and if they allow us to do it at Royal Ascot I'd love to take her to the Duke of Cambridge Stakes," said Walker. "This was a crucial first win at Listed level."

Aljazzi is the most notable recent winner of the Snowdrop, landing the race in 2017 before finishing second to Qemah in the Duke of Cambridge and then winning the Royal Ascot race last year.

HERMOSA

"She's a very, very, very tough filly." Aidan O'Brien could not have stated more emphatically his admiration for Hermosa's resilience after her all-the-way win in the 1,000 Guineas at Newmarket, which opened up a range of options for a prolonged campaign at Group 1 level. The Royal Ascot target would be the Coronation Stakes for a double attempted by two of O'Brien's previous four Guineas winners and completed only by Winter in 2017. Perhaps Hermosa's style of running would make her vulnerable to a finisher up Ascot's short straight but she wouldn't be easy to pass.

LADY KAYA

Lady Kaya ran a stormer to finish second behind Hermosa in the 1,000 Guineas but trainer Sheila Lavery *(right, with her stable star)* was quick to look at a drop back in trip for the Commonwealth Cup, which in its short history has become such an attractive Group 1 option for three-year-olds who do not truly see out a mile.

Lavery, who trains the Dandy Man filly for her niece Joanne, said: "She ran an absolute cracker [at Newmarket] and I couldn't be prouder of her. I never let myself dream at any stage during the race as we all knew she had to get home over a mile. She travelled beautifully through the race and the plan now is to drop her to six furlongs and have a go at the Commonwealth Cup. She has loads of speed, so a stiff six furlongs at Ascot should really suit her."

FAIRYLAND

Aidan O'Brien's three-year-old was fifth behind stablemate Hermosa in the 1,000 Guineas but would not be the first to bounce back from disappointment there if she heads to the Coronation Stakes at Royal Ascot. Five of the last eight Coronation winners who had run in the Newmarket Classic had not won there, with four of those finishing out of the places.

The alternative is to go back to sprinting with the Kodiac filly, who showed her speed last season by winning the Group 2 Lowther and Group 1 Cheveley Park and had never raced beyond 6f before the Guineas.

JUVENILE CONTENDERS

Matt Butler investigates which tracks have been the best starting points for recent Royal Ascot two-year-old winners

Does it matter where you start? With two-year-old winners at Royal Ascot (including the year it was relocated to York) debuting at 37 different tracks in two continents and five countries since the start of the century, the figures may suggest it does not. However, like life in general, there can be a significant advantage to starting life in more esteemed surroundings, and these are the tracks that have most often paved the way to Royal Ascot success

Shang Shang Shang (yellow cap) started at Keeneland before last year's Norfolk win

NEWMARKET – ROWLEY MILE COURSE DEBUT VENUE FOR 11 ROYAL ASCOT WINNERS SINCE 2000

This has been a particularly good starting point for Albany winners (four of them – Sander Camillo, Habaayib, Samitar and Kiyoshi), although the competitiveness of Newmarket races is underlined by the fact that none of them won on debut (only four of the 11 Royal Ascot winners who started here did so). Three more Royal Ascot-winning

juveniles started a bit later on the July course.

WINDSOR NINE ROYAL ASCOT WINNERS

Racecourses can dip in and out of fashion, with Windsor not quite as popular for smart two-year-olds making their debuts as it used to be, although Main Edition's Albany win last year could signal a changing of the tide again. The Berkshire track used to be an excellent location to spot Windsor Castle winners in particular – four (Autumnal, Chateau Istana, Elhamri and Flashmans Papers) debuted here between 2000 and 2008.

Analysis

NEWBURY NINE ROYAL ASCOT WINNERS

Newbury is another Berkshire course to prove less popular than it was in the noughties, although Advertise went close to improving the track's recent record when second in last year's Coventry. Three consecutive Chesham winners (Whazzat, Championship Point and Champlain) debuted at Newbury between 2004 and 2006 – and it's worth noting that all nine who started here finished in the first three.

CURRAGH FIVE ROYAL ASCOT WINNERS

The Curragh was not always a popular starting point for two-year-olds, with all five winners coming since 2011. As at Newmarket, do not count on them being successful first time out. That is unless they are destined for the Coventry, with

Main Edition's victory in last season's Albany followed her Windsor debut

Classic winners Power and Dawn Approach announcing their significant ability from the very start.

KEENELAND FIVE ROYAL ASCOT WINNERS

Wesley Ward is the reason for the Kentucky track's presence on this list. His trailblazer Jealous Again won on her debut here before landing the 2009 Queen Mary, the brilliant Lady Aurelia did likewise in 2016, and last year Shang Shang Shang had one winning run at Keeneland before her Norfolk success.

KEMPTON FIVE ROYAL ASCOT WINNERS

Kempton's total is a combination of debuts on the all-weather track and the now defunct Flat turf course. Good horses have always used Kempton's Polytrack, be it juveniles or older horses,

and its record of hosting Royal Ascot winners on their debuts – 2014 Albany scorer Cursory Glance was the most recent – adds to the list of reasons why it would be a massive shame if the track ultimately succumbed to developers.

NAAS FIVE ROYAL ASCOT WINNERS

Naas shares top billing with the Curragh as the best starting point in Ireland for a Royal Ascot juvenile. Three of the track's juvenile success stories – Brave Anna, Sioux Nation and Maybe – were trained by Aidan O'Brien, with Cuis Ghaire and Elletelle completing the quintet.

BEST OF THE REST

Sandown and Nottingham are next best with four winners, although 2010 Queen Mary winner Maqaasid was Sandown's most recent.

Eight tracks have provided three winners, including Ayr and Hamilton in Scotland and Leopardstown in Ireland.

Ascot itself was the starting place for two winners – note that neither made their debut at the royal meeting – while a further ten tracks, including Churchill Downs and Dundalk, also provided two.

JUVENILE CONTENDERS

MONARCH OF EGYPT

The first juvenile Aidan O'Brien ran this season could end up being one of the most exciting for the remainder of the campaign. A $750,000 first-crop son of US Triple Crown hero American Pharoah, Monarch Of Egypt backed up his pedigree sheet with a dominant debut victory at Naas. That came over 5f but he immediately went into the reckoning for the Coventry Stakes with O'Brien saying there would be "no problem getting 6f or 7f". The trainer added: "He's uncomplicated. He's a straightforward and honest horse who has been showing us plenty on the gallops at home."

CHASING DREAMS

Charlie Appleby could have a strong team of juveniles at the royal meeting (including Expressionist, Well Of Wisdom and Full Verse) but the pick of them might be this Starspangledbanner filly, who cruised home by five lengths on her debut at Newmarket's Craven meeting. That form has already worked out well, with runner-up Good Vibes also confirming herself a good prospect with her Listed Marygate Stakes victory at York's May

meeting, and the Queen Mary is an obvious target for Appleby's exciting filly.

NAYIBETH

Usually it pays to take note when US trainer Wesley Ward nominates one of his Royal Ascot team as "the pick of our two-year-olds". That was the tag he gave to Nayibeth following her

debut victory in an electrifying time over 4½f at Keeneland in April, the same preparation used for his standout Royal Ascot winner Lady Aurelia before her runaway Queen Mary success in 2016. With Lady Pauline earmarked for that race this year, Ward has a different target in mind for Nayibeth. "She won nicely

Six to watch

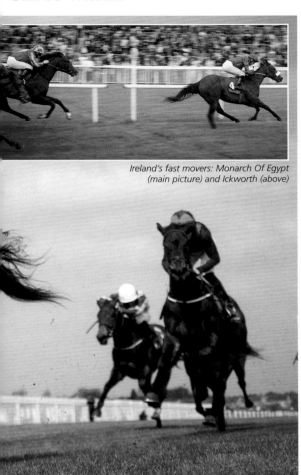

Ireland's fast movers: Monarch Of Egypt (main picture) and Ickworth (above)

possibly the Windsor Castle, the race in which Watson broke his royal duck last year with Soldier's Call.

KEMBLE

Having finished third to fellow Royal Ascot possible Chasing Dreams on her debut, this Richard Hannon-trained filly showed the benefit of that experience with an impressive victory at Windsor next time. She beat a solid yardstick in Illusionist by five lengths and looks well worth a crack in Group company. She has the speed to go for the Queen Mary but could potentially stay a furlong further and try for the Albany.

ICKWORTH

Godolphin look so strong in the juvenile department, and Ickworth was so impressive in 5f Listed victory at the Curragh in early May, that this daughter of Shamardal took high rank in the ante-post betting for the Coventry (against the colts) as well as the Queen Mary. The February foal was precocious enough to make her winning debut in late March at Dundalk and trainer Willie McCreery is excited about the next step, probably in the Queen Mary. "It's always a stiff five [at the Curragh] and I'd be thinking of five rather than six for her at the moment," he said.

on debut and I think we're going to go for the Albany. It's not a race I've won yet but she's very smart," he said.

ELECTRIC LADYLAND

Archie Watson has been the trainer to follow with early juveniles, sending out several first-time winners. Among them is Electric Ladyland,

who blazed home twice on the all-weather from wide draws. Her bad luck with the stalls continued at Chester when she was posted widest of all in the Lily Agnes and she could finish only sixth of seven after an awkward start. That run is easily forgiven and a good draw and quick ground at Ascot could make her tough to catch in

JUVENILE CONTENDERS

THREAT

Richard Hannon has sent out scores of juvenile winners but is yet to claim the Coventry Stakes, a race his father won three times including back-to-back successes in 2009 and 2010 with Canford Cliffs and Strong Suit.

Threat looks set to live up to his name, having made a clear-cut winning start in a warm-looking maiden at Newmarket. That was over 5f but Hannon immediately nominated the Coventry for the son of Footstepsinthesand, saying: "If our two-year-olds win first time out, generally they're very good – and if they win like that, it's a great sign."

LADY PAULINE

Wesley Ward's speedsters have become a feature of the royal meeting and the American trainer gave Lady Pauline an early taste of the track on trials day at the start of May.

She was long odds-on to win that day, having hosed up back home over 4½f at Keeneland, but could not finish off her race having shown blistering early speed.

Connections felt the Ascot race came quick enough after her flight to Britain and she remains interesting, especially as she is a half-sister to dual Royal Ascot winner Lady Aurelia.

VENTURA REBEL

Ventura Rebel has shown smart form over 5f for Richard Fahey, stepping up on a debut win at Thirsk to beat Lady Pauline at Ascot.

A case can be made for that form being suspect as the favourite failed to run to expectations but Tom Palin, syndicate manager for owners Middleham Park Racing, said: "The time he did suggests he should be in the mix in the Norfolk, but the visual impression he gave suggests six furlongs [in the Coventry] shouldn't be a problem."

FULL AUTHORITY

David O'Meara made his reputation by improving horses from other yards but he has put greater focus on juveniles this year and it is paying off, with this son of Kingman leading the charge.

He was favourite for his debut over 5f at Chester's May meeting, having drawn well in stall three, and his six-length victory could not have been more impressive.

"If we had any concern it

Six more to watch

Shows of strength: Ventura Rebel (left) defeats Lady Pauline at Ascot; Full Authority (above) scores at Chester; Siskin wins in good style at Naas

was the soft ground first time out but he coped with it fine," O'Meara said. "I can't imagine he'll be inconvenienced by quicker ground. The owner loves Ascot and if the horse is well he'll take his chance in one of the races."

SISKIN

Ger Lyons was entrusted with this Juddmonte homebred and the February foal made a flying start with a debut victory over 6f at Naas in May, scoring by two and three-quarter lengths to put himself in the Coventry Stakes reckoning.

"He's just shown what we've seen of him on the gallops," Lyons said. "Most of our two-year-olds this year are quite backward but not this fellow.

"He's very straightforward and quick. There will be plenty of physical improvement too."

FINAL SONG

Only three of Saeed Bin Suroor's 36 Royal Ascot victories have been with two-year-olds but Final Song, his first juvenile winner of the season at Ascot, looks a live contender after an impressive start over 5f. The daughter of Dark Angel has a speedy pedigree full of juvenile winners and she skipped clear by five lengths on soft ground.

The Queen Mary looked the obvious target but Bin Suroor said: "I think she wants six furlongs and nice ground – I think it will be the Albany. She's always shown plenty of class at home."

THE INTERNATIONAL CHALLENGE

Global aces: trainer Lee Freedman (left) and the Miss Andretti team celebrate their win in the 2007 King's Stand Stakes; (clockwise from top left on facing page) No Nay Never, Choisir, Acapulco, Strike The Tiger, Little Bridge, Undrafted, Hootenanny, Jealous Again and Scenic Blast

ROYAL ASCOT has long been renowned across the world but less than 20 years ago it was a purely European occasion with its runners drawn largely from Britain and Ireland, plus a healthy sprinkling of French stars to add continental glamour.

Then in 2002 came two important changes that were to change the face of the royal meeting. First the fixture expanded from four to five days, and at the same time Ascot actively started looking further afield for runners.

That policy paid

immediate dividends. In 2003 there were eight runners from outside Europe – coming from the United States, Australia, Hong Kong, South Africa and the United Arab Emirates – and one of them, the incredible Aussie sprinter Choisir, took the meeting by storm with

'In 2002 came two important changes that were to change the face of the royal meeting. First the fixture expanded from four to five days, and at the same time Ascot actively started looking further afield for runners'

double success in the King's Stand Stakes on the Tuesday and the Golden Jubilee Stakes on the Saturday.

The following year there was no winner from outside Europe but Hong Kong's Cape Of Good Hope was second in the King's Stand and returned 12 months ▶

THE INTERNATIONAL CHALLENGE

later to land that race when the royal meeting was switched to York.

Three more Group 1 sprints went to Australia by 2009 and in that same year there was a fresh twist to the raiding party when US trainer Wesley Ward started to bring his precocious, speedy two-year-olds to the meeting. Again it was immediately successful as Ward took the Queen Mary Stakes with Jealous Again and the Windsor Castle Stakes with Strike The Tiger.

Fast-forward a decade and the score for non-European raiders now stands at 19 – a strike-rate of around one winner per year – and their impact continues to be felt most strongly in the Group 1 sprints open to older horses (ten wins) and two-year-old races (seven). Non-Europeans have won 15 per

cent of those races since 2003 – a remarkable figure considering the record number for the raiding party in a single year is 15 in 2015.

Ward has become the mainstay in recent years and is sure to have a powerful team again, but other American trainers who made Group 1 entries this year are Peter Miller (Stormy Liberal, Diamond Jubilee Stakes), Chad Brown (Newspaperofrecord, Coronation Stakes), Joe Orseno (Imprimis, King's

Stand and Diamond Jubilee Stakes), Ari Herbertson (Tribal Storm, King's Stand), Todd Pletcher (Bulletin, St James's Palace Stakes and Commonwealth Cup), Brendan Walsh (Uncapped, Commonwealth Cup) and Ben Colebrook (Fancy Dress Party, Commonwealth Cup).

With Japanese star mare Deirdre heading for the Prince of Wales's Stakes and Australian sprinters Zousain and Houtzen in the mix, international interest remains strong.

'Ward has become the mainstay in recent years and is sure to have a powerful team again'

*Stormy Liberal:
US entry a sign of
continuing interest*

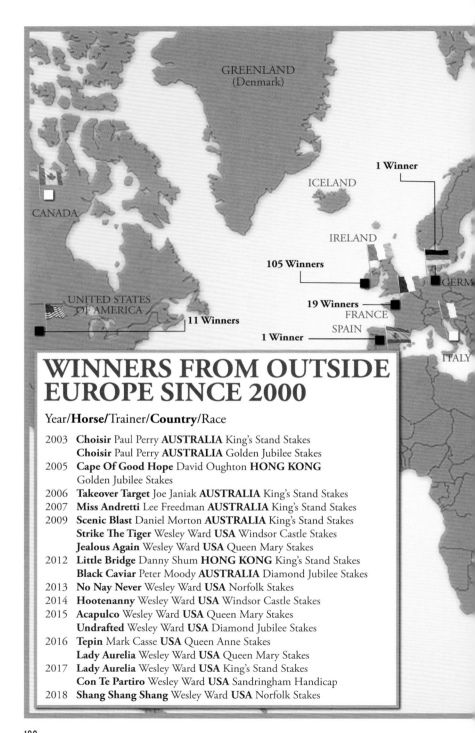

GREENLAND
(Denmark)

1 Winner

ICELAND

CANADA

IRELAND

105 Winners

GERM

UNITED STATES
OF AMERICA

19 Winners
FRANCE

11 Winners

SPAIN

1 Winner

ITALY

WINNERS FROM OUTSIDE EUROPE SINCE 2000

Year/**Horse**/Trainer/**Country**/Race

2003   **Choisir** Paul Perry **AUSTRALIA** King's Stand Stakes
       Choisir Paul Perry **AUSTRALIA** Golden Jubilee Stakes
2005   **Cape Of Good Hope** David Oughton **HONG KONG**
       Golden Jubilee Stakes
2006   **Takeover Target** Joe Janiak **AUSTRALIA** King's Stand Stakes
2007   **Miss Andretti** Lee Freedman **AUSTRALIA** King's Stand Stakes
2009   **Scenic Blast** Daniel Morton **AUSTRALIA** King's Stand Stakes
       Strike The Tiger Wesley Ward **USA** Windsor Castle Stakes
       Jealous Again Wesley Ward **USA** Queen Mary Stakes
2012   **Little Bridge** Danny Shum **HONG KONG** King's Stand Stakes
       Black Caviar Peter Moody **AUSTRALIA** Diamond Jubilee Stakes
2013   **No Nay Never** Wesley Ward **USA** Norfolk Stakes
2014   **Hootenanny** Wesley Ward **USA** Windsor Castle Stakes
2015   **Acapulco** Wesley Ward **USA** Queen Mary Stakes
       Undrafted Wesley Ward **USA** Diamond Jubilee Stakes
2016   **Tepin** Mark Casse **USA** Queen Anne Stakes
       Lady Aurelia Wesley Ward **USA** Queen Mary Stakes
2017   **Lady Aurelia** Wesley Ward **USA** King's Stand Stakes
       Con Te Partiro Wesley Ward **USA** Sandringham Handicap
2018   **Shang Shang Shang** Wesley Ward **USA** Norfolk Stakes

WORLD-CLASS COMPETITION

Overseas-trained runners at Royal Ascot since 2000

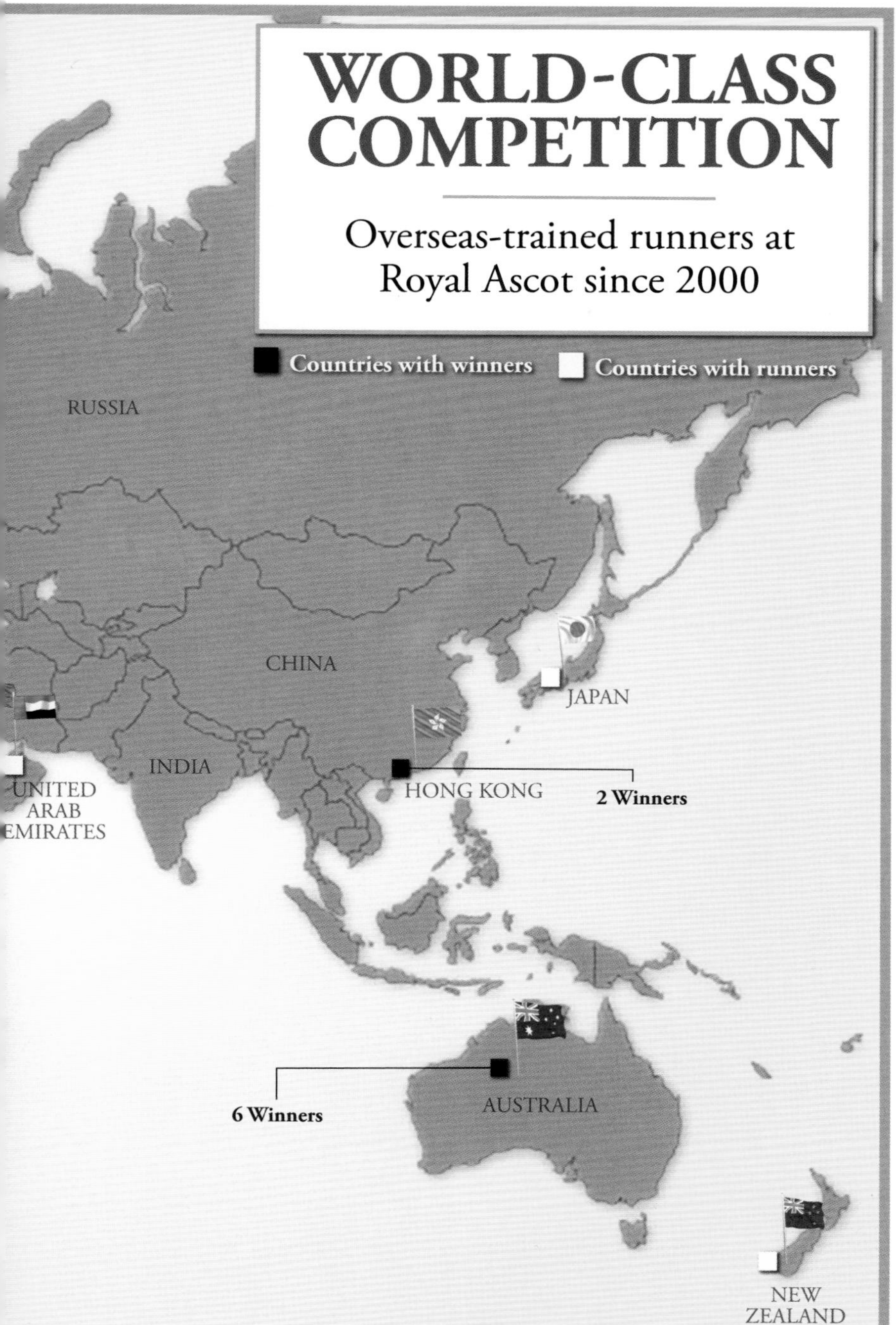

■ **Countries with winners**   □ **Countries with runners**

RUSSIA

CHINA

JAPAN

INDIA

HONG KONG   **2 Winners**

UNITED
ARAB
EMIRATES

AUSTRALIA

6 Winners

NEW
ZEALAND

Rocky year in love affair

FRANCE had a rare blank at Royal Ascot last year but the raiders were competitive, going agonisingly close in two of the biggest races when Vazirabad lost out by three-quarters of a length in the Gold Cup and City Light was just held by a short head in the Diamond Jubilee Stakes.

Those near-misses left French trainers without a win for only the seventh time at the last 20 Royal Ascots but their long-term strike-rate is so good that the drought is unlikely to last long.

In the three years before last year's blank, France had eight winners at a strike-rate of 15 per cent for a level-stake profit of +6.19pt.

OUTRIGHT FAVOURITES HAVE HIGH STRIKE-RATE

TOP TIPS

STRONG RECORD IN FILLIES-ONLY RACES

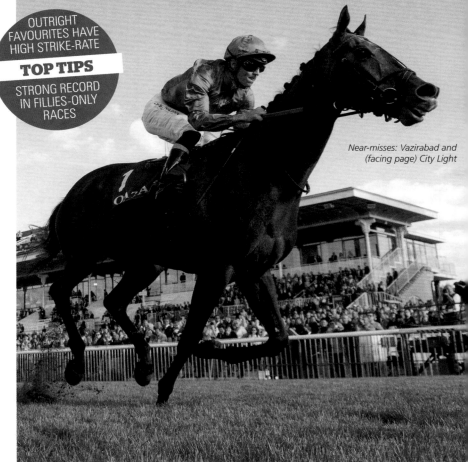

Near-misses: Vazirabad and (facing page) City Light

French trainers

Despite that profit figure, backing blind is not the best policy and there are more nuanced ways of making money on French runners.

One is to be price-sensitive and concentrate only on runners who are well fancied in the betting market. By definition, those are the runners with the best form and it is notable that four of the eight French winners in the three years from 2015 to 2017 went off favourite and another was second favourite. Not only

that, but that quartet were the only French-trained outright favourites in those three years, producing a 100 per cent strike-rate and a level-stake profit of +8.13pt.

Overall, since 2000, eight of the 17 French-trained outright favourites have been successful (47%, +6.64pt).

Last year, perhaps significantly, France did not have a single favourite and nothing shorter than Vazirabad at 9-2.

Another way of narrowing down the French challenge is to focus on the fillies. Five of their eight winners in 2015-17 came in races restricted to fillies and mares (27%, +20.75pt) and perhaps that is because these divisions lack some depth and French trainers send only their best-regarded fillies.

On the trainer front, Andre Fabre always has to be respected (two winners, a second and a third from seven runners in the past five years) and Jean-Claude Rouget (left) is similarly strong now (three winners and a second from six runners in the same period).

Japanese mare with royal links

JAPANESE horses have won big races across the globe, including the Dubai World Cup and Melbourne Cup, and this year's big hope to break their duck at Royal Ascot is seasoned globetrotter Deirdre, who is set to go for the Prince of Wales's Stakes.

The Group 1-winning mare arrived in Britain at the start of May to begin her final preparations in Newmarket, having shipped from Hong Kong following her sixth place in the Group 1 Queen Elizabeth II Cup over the same 1m2f trip as the Prince of Wales's. Before that she had been fourth behind world-class compatriot Almond Eye in the 1m1f Group 1 Dubai Turf on World Cup night at Meydan.

Ascot took the gamble of closing entries for the Group 1 races a week later this year, allowing horses to run on Champions Day in Hong Kong before committing to travel, and it has paid off with Deirdre's scheduled appearance.

"Japanese horses are fundamental and the key thing was to get Deirdre for the Prince of Wales's," said Ascot director of racing and communications Nick Smith. "Changing the entry date and pushing it back a week really worked in terms of bringing the Japanese horse over after running at Sha Tin."

The Prince of Wales's is right at the top end of global competition and Deirdre's peak Racing Post Rating of 114 – achieved in her Group 1 Shuka Sho victory in October 2017 and again in a Group 2 win on home soil last autumn – gives her plenty to find, but there are some positive indicators.

In her first overseas run, in the 2018 Dubai Turf, she was third to Godolphin's three-time Group 1 winner Benbatl, while in this year's contest she was just behind Lord Glitters (runner-up in last year's Queen Anne Stakes) and just ahead of Without Parole, last year's St James's Palace Stakes winner.

The five-year-old has Royal Ascot in her blood, as her sire is 2010 Hardwicke Stakes winner Harbinger, who went on to even better on the course with his King George VI and Queen Elizabeth Stakes victory.

She has Japanese racing royalty in the saddle, with Yutaka Take having recently taken up the reins. Take, 50, who last year became the first Japanese rider to reach 4,000 winners, has an excellent big-race pedigree, including 2000 July Cup victory on Agnes World.

STAR RATING
★ ★ ★

Deirdre heads for the Prince of Wales's Stakes, bidding to emulate her Royal Ascot-winning sire Harbinger, who took the Hardwicke Stakes (facing page)

US ace bidding to make

'BOUND for Royal Ascot' has become the regular tag attached to Bound For Nowhere in early summer and Wesley Ward's tough and speedy five-year-old has justified his previous trips with two high-class runs in Group 1 contests.

In 2017 he was fourth behind Caravaggio, Harry Angel and Blue Point in a red-hot edition of the Commonwealth Cup and last year he was beaten only three-quarters of a length into third by Merchant Navy and City Light in the Diamond Jubilee Stakes.

The Diamond Jubilee is likely to be the target again

over the six-furlong trip he has handled so well on his previous visits. He has plenty of speed, having pulled his way to the front in last year's race, and showed his stamina with a Listed win over a mile in Kentucky last September. That is a potent combination when it comes to the demands of an uphill finish off a fast pace at the royal meeting.

Ward has chosen the same Grade 2 contest at Keeneland in early April for Bound For Nowhere's prep in

Wesley Ward: pleased with Keeneland prep run

2018 and 2019 and, while this year's runner-up effort looked disappointing in comparison to his four-length win 12 months earlier, the trainer was satisfied with the run under jockey Luis Saez.

"Bound For Nowhere ran really well when second at Keeneland," said Ward. "The race was quite tactical and he had a new rider on. We made all, whereas we usually hold him up. That race did him the world of good. The only other time he has raced up with the pace was when he came third in the Diamond Jubilee, which was a fine effort."

Ward won the Diamond Jubilee with Undrafted in 2015 – the trainer's first Royal Ascot success outside juvenile company – and Bound For Nowhere has a similar profile, arguably even better. Undrafted had already gone well in a British Group 1 sprint (fourth in the 2014 July Cup) and reached a Racing Post Rating of 118, whereas Bound For Nowhere has RPRs of 121 and 119 on his record.

it third time lucky

As a five-year-old Undrafted hit his peak with an RPR of 123 for his Diamond Jubilee success, proving Ward's ability to keep improving a battle-hardened sprinter. Royal glory is within reach again if the shrewd trainer can eke out that little extra from Bound For Nowhere.

Bound For Nowhere finishes fourth to Caravaggio in the Commonwealth Cup before improving a place to take third in last year's Diamond Jubilee Stakes (below, second right)

STAR RATING
★★★★

Delve deep for profits

LAST year Aidan O'Brien was leading trainer at Royal Ascot for the fourth year in a row, and the ninth time in all, although his total of four winners was lower than in recent years and he had only one Group 1 success, with Merchant Navy in the Diamond Jubilee Stakes.

That just goes to show the high level of competition at Royal Ascot even for a trainer as powerful as O'Brien. All five of his favourites were beaten at last year's meeting, although in general his best chances are well indicated in the market. None of his 2018 winners was bigger than 5-1 and 31 of his 39 winners (79%) in the past decade have been priced below 8-1.

Backing all his favourites in the past decade would have yielded a small profit (37%, +3.17pt) but mainly because of a couple of bigger-priced winners near the start of the period. His market leaders tend to go off shorter nowadays and one notable factor is that all his successful favourites in Group 1s since 2012 were odds-on.

The best place to find a longer-priced O'Brien winner is in one of the races restricted to a single age group – two-year-olds or three-year-olds. All eight of his winners in the past decade priced in double figures fitted that criterion.

It is slightly unexpected that Ryan Moore was aboard three of those eight, as was Seamie Heffernan.

Four of the eight came in juvenile races, including two of the last four Norfolk Stakes (Waterloo Bridge at 12-1 and Sioux Nation at 14-1) when the winner was the stable's only representative and was ridden by Moore.

O'Brien has had only eight runners in the Norfolk since 2010, and never more than one a year, but apart from the two winners he has had two seconds, a third and a fourth.

RACES OVER MIDDLE DISTANCES A STRONG POINT

TOP TIPS

LOOK AT NORFOLK AND JERSEY RUNNERS

Hunting Horn gives Aidan O'Brien one of last year's four successes

O'BRIEN'S ROYAL ASCOT WINNERS BY AGE GROUP

- 3yo **28**
- 4yo+ **20**
- 2yo **17**

Moore is also worth noting when he has a handicap ride for O'Brien. The trainer has had two wins from 16 runners in that sphere since 2015 and it is notable that both were the only runners in their respective races and were ridden by Moore, returning SPs of 7-1 and 10-1. Moore had just nine rides in handicaps for O'Brien in that timeframe, with one other placed at 7-1.

Another race where O'Brien could turn up a big-priced chance is the Jersey Stakes, with one of his three-year-olds who may not have made the top grade in miling or sprinting. From 13 runners

1997 YEAR OF FIRST ROYAL ASCOT WINNER

in the past decade, he has had two winners (at 20-1 and 9-2), a 66-1 second and two thirds (one at 14-1).

The Group races for middle-distance/staying types are a strong point. In the past decade he has had five winners in the Queen's Vase, three in the Ribblesdale Stakes and two in the Hardwicke Stakes (10-40, 25%, +32.45pt in those three races). In addition, while his only winner of the King Edward VII Stakes was Five Dynasties in 2004, his runners often go well (12 out of 15 have been in the first four in the past decade).

MOST SUCCESSFUL RACES

Coventry Stakes
■■■■■■■■

Gold Cup
■■■■■■■

St James's Palace Stakes
■■■■■■■

Queen's Vase
■■■■■■

Chesham Stakes
■■■■

Coronation Stakes
■■■

Hampton Court Stakes
■■■

Hardwicke Stakes
■■■

Jersey Stakes
■■■

Norfolk Stakes
■■■

Prince of Wales's Stakes
■■■

Queen Anne Stakes
■■■

Ribblesdale Stakes
■■■

65
ROYAL ASCOT WINNERS

21
DIFFERENT RACES WON

9
TOP TRAINER AWARDS

Great staying power

NOT so long ago Sir Michael Stoute seemed to be a fading force but he was back to his brilliant best at Royal Ascot 2018 with four winners, spearheaded by Group 1 scorers Poet's Word in the Prince of Wales's Stakes and Eqtidaar in the Commonwealth Cup. His other two winners – Crystal Ocean (Hardwicke Stakes) and Expert Eye (Jersey Stakes) – also came in Group races.

That took the ten-time champion to the outright record for Royal Ascot winners with 79 – four clear of the late, great Sir Henry Cecil – and it was possibly the best royal meeting of his long career, considering he has never exceeded four winners (a feat he has now achieved on five occasions) and had won only two of the Group 1 contests in the preceding 15 years.

The Newmarket trainer's first Royal Ascot winner came in the 1977 Jersey Stakes with Etienne Gerard, five years after he had started training, and his record has been a

MOST SUCCESSFUL RACES

Hardwicke Stakes
■■■■■■■■■■■
King Edward VII Stakes
■■■■■■■
Duke of Edinburgh Stakes
■■■■■■
Jersey Stakes
■■■■■■
King George V Handicap
■■■■■
Britannia Handicap
■■■■
Coronation Stakes
■■■■
Duke of Cambridge Stakes
■■■■
Queen's Vase
■■■■
Prince of Wales's Stakes
■■■
Queen Anne Stakes
■■■
Ribblesdale Stakes
■■■

STOUTE'S ROYAL ASCOT WINNERS BY DISTANCE

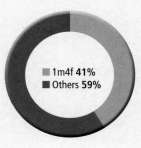

■ 1m4f **41%**
■ Others **59%**

model of consistency. He has been top trainer at the meeting six times and has had only seven blanks in the 42 years since his first success.

Even so, before last year's glorious resurgence, he had come to rely on a handful of races for the bulk of his winners since 2004 – the Hardwicke (seven), the Duke of Edinburgh Handicap (four), the Duke of Cambridge Stakes (four) and the King Edward VII Stakes (three).

Those four races still account for more than half of his winners at the past 15 meetings and they are likely to remain his strong points.

What is notable about those favourite races is that three of the four are run at 1m4f. The exception is the Duke of Cambridge Stakes over a mile, although that race is for fillies and mares – a department where Stoute also tends to be well stocked. Until last year's wins with Eqtidaar and Expert Eye, he hadn't scored with a male runner at less than 1m2f since Jeremy took the 7f Jersey Stakes in 2006.

TOP TIPS

TAKE NOTE OF FILLIES BELOW GROUP 1 LEVEL

LOOK TO OLDER HORSES OVER 1M4F

79
ROYAL ASCOT WINNERS

9
SUCCESSFUL FAVOURITES AMONG LAST 17 WINNERS

4
WINNERS LAST YEAR, HIS JOINT-BEST HAUL

1977
YEAR OF FIRST ROYAL ASCOT WINNER

Market a good guide

JOHN GOSDEN is second only to Aidan O'Brien on the Royal Ascot honours board for the past five seasons, having saddled 14 winners to his Irish rival's 24 (next after Gosden is Sir Michael Stoute on 11), and his power and influence continue to grow.

Last year Gosden had four winners headed by Group 1 stars Stradivarius in the Gold Cup and Without Parole in the St James's Palace Stakes, backed up by Calyx in the Coventry Stakes and Monarchs Glen in the Wolferton Stakes. He finished level with O'Brien and Stoute for wins but the leading trainer award went to O'Brien by virtue of his greater number of runners-up.

It was the third time in seven years that Gosden (below) had sent out at least four winners (his best was five in 2012) and his overall total now stands at 47, having more than doubled in the past decade.

Given that Gosden has plenty of runners, the key for punters is to find ways of narrowing the focus. One angle is that his record with fancied runners is pretty good. Since 2010, 14 of his 23 winners have been priced at 6-1 or below, from 40 runners in that category (35%, +13.73pt). Much of the profit comes from his standout year in 2012, although there has not been a significant loss in any of those years by following his shorter-priced runners.

It is worth noting that all but one of Gosden's other nine winners since 2010 were priced at 8-1 to 12-1 (and all in that bracket were in the first six in the market), emphasising that it is rare for him to win with an outsider.

His handicap favourites are well worth watching, as four of his six winners in that sphere in the past decade headed the market. He had just eight handicap favourites in that period, which works out at a 50% strike-rate and a level-stake profit of +8pt, and that is even after last year's finger-burning for punters when 2-1 hotpot Dreamfield was second in the Wokingham.

Gosden is known for his patient handling of horses and it is often a good sign when he has a two-year-old ready to run at the meeting. He has had just 14 juvenile runners since 2010 but five have won, at odds of 7-4, 2-1, 9-4, 10-1 and 20-1 (36%, +27pt).

MOST SUCCESSFUL RACES

Britannia Handicap
■■■■
Wolferton Stakes
■■■■
Chesham Stakes
■■■
King Edward VII Stakes
■■■
Prince of Wales's Stakes
■■■

GOSDEN'S ROYAL ASCOT WINNERS BY DISTANCE (2009-)

- ■ 1m/1m2f
- ■ 1m4f/1m6f
- ■ 5-7f
- ■ 2m4f

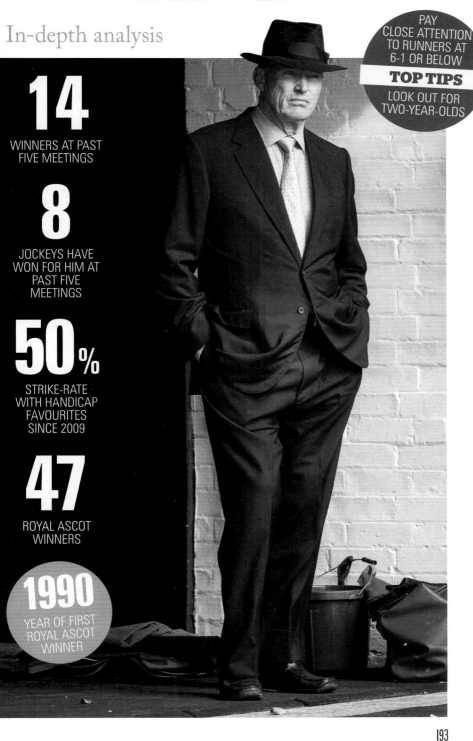

PAY CLOSE ATTENTION TO RUNNERS AT 6-1 OR BELOW

TOP TIPS

LOOK OUT FOR TWO-YEAR-OLDS

14
WINNERS AT PAST FIVE MEETINGS

8
JOCKEYS HAVE WON FOR HIM AT PAST FIVE MEETINGS

50%
STRIKE-RATE WITH HANDICAP FAVOURITES SINCE 2009

47
ROYAL ASCOT WINNERS

1990
YEAR OF FIRST ROYAL ASCOT WINNER

Juveniles worth a look

GODOLPHIN enjoyed a resurgence across the globe in 2018, winning two of the most cherished prizes in the Derby and the Melbourne Cup, and it was no different at Royal Ascot.

Charlie Appleby, who has taken over the lead trainer role from Saeed Bin Suroor, struck with Blue Point in the King's Stand Stakes – a first Group 1 winner at the meeting since 2012 from Godolphin's own Newmarket stables – and Old Persian in the Group 2 King Edward VII Stakes.

That took Appleby to six winners in five Royal Ascots since he stepped up from his previous job as assistant and his pre-eminence at Godolphin is clear from the fact that Bin Suroor has had just two winners in the same period.

Appleby also had Derby winner Masar and

Point made: a punch of the air from William Buick after Blue Point's success in last year's King's Stand Stakes for Charlie Appleby (facing page). The balance of power has swung in Appleby's favour and away from Saeed Bin Suroor (right)

Melbourne Cup scorer Cross Counter in 2018, emphasising how the balance of power has swung in his favour.

Godolphin has also diversified away from its private yards and seven other trainers have got on the scoreboard under the blue banner at the past six Royal Ascots – four from Britain (Richard Fahey, Richard Hannon, Mark Johnston and Roger Charlton), two from Ireland (Jim Bolger and Mick Halford) and Andre Fabre from France.

None of the 'outside' trainers was successful last year but perhaps they are able to be more selective with their runners and it is worth noting that in 2016 and 2017 they had six winners from 34 (18%, +1.85pt), which improved slightly when excluding two-year-olds (generally not a Godolphin strong point early in the season).

Juvenile success is most likely to come from Appleby, who has proved adept at targeting a handful of two-year-olds at the meeting. In the past two years he has had a 16-1 winner, two seconds, a third and a fourth from just eight juvenile runners. He seems to have a strong team this year.

Handicaps can be another fruitful area, with Appleby also targeting these races more carefully. In the past two years six of his 16 handicap runners have made the first four, often rewarding each-way support at big odds, with one winning at 20-1.

The Royal Hunt Cup, King George V and Duke of Edinburgh are the three handicaps to watch with the two Godolphin trainers. In the last five years, they have had nine horses win or place in those three races at odds ranging from 4-1 to 33-1.

Bin Suroor has been leading trainer at Royal Ascot four times and his strength has been older horses, with only three of his 36 winners coming in two-year-old races. Two of those three juvenile wins were in the Chesham Stakes, so note any runners there, although it is fair to say he is not the force of old.

LOOK OUT FOR CHARLIE APPLEBY JUVENILES

TOP TIPS

HANDICAPPERS OFTEN SCORE AT GOOD ODDS

Success in the long run

MARK JOHNSTON is fourth on the list of top current trainers at Royal Ascot, with only Sir Michael Stoute, Aidan O'Brien and John Gosden ahead of him, and he took his score to 43 last year with wins from Baghdad in the King George V Handicap and Main Edition in the Albany Stakes.

That was Johnston's fourth double in five years – the exception was a rare blank in 2016 – and he continues to be one of the meeting's most reliable performers even though he does not receive the same high-quality intake of his major rivals.

Johnston, who later in the summer of 2018 became the winningmost British trainer of all time when he reached the 4,194 mark, has enjoyed most of his Royal Ascot success in the longer-distance events and it was no surprise that he opened his account last year in the King George V over 1m4f.

His score in that race now stands at six, alongside multiple victories in the Gold Cup, Hardwicke Stakes, Duke of Edinburgh Handicap, Queen's Vase, King Edward VII Stakes and Queen Alexandra Stakes.

Twenty-nine of his 43 winners have been at 1m4f-plus and his runners are always worth a close look in the races where stamina and fitness are paramount. Last year he had 9-1 winner Baghdad from nine runners in that category and the year before it was two from nine (22%, +9pt) with Permian (King Edward VII, 1m4f) and Oriental Fox (Queen Alexandra, 2m5½f).

In the past decade, ten of Johnston's 89 runners at 1m4f-plus have been successful at a strike-rate of 11 per cent and a small level-stake loss. What is most notable is that six of those winners were ridden by Joe Fanning from 30 rides (20%, +26.5pt).

A strong showing with a two-year-old is not out of the question, especially with a fancied runner like 7-1 shot Main Edition last year. Johnston has had 15 juveniles priced at 10-1 or below in the past decade for two winners, a second, a third and two fourths.

Baghdad (centre) gets up to win last year's King George V Handicap

STRONG ACROSS THE BOARD AT 1M4F-PLUS

TOP TIPS

JOE FANNING IS THE KEY RIDER IN THOSE RACES

Wesley Ward

Premium on speed

FEW individual trainers change the face of racing as much as Ward, who has almost single-handedly added a colourful American dimension to Royal Ascot since he first took the meeting by storm in 2009 with a pair of lightning-fast two-year-old winners in Jealous Again (Queen Mary Stakes) and Strike The Tiger (Windsor Castle Stakes).

The US trainer has missed only one year since and, although he had to wait until 2013 to strike again, he has continued to leave a significant imprint on the meeting. He has had at least one winner every year since 2013 and last year's success came in the Norfolk Stakes with Shang Shang Shang, another flying two-year-old.

Ward's total now stands at ten, a score bettered by only a dozen current British or Irish trainers, and

he ranks fifth on the Royal Ascot scoreboard over the past five years. Eight of those ten wins have come over five furlongs, which suits his fast horses ideally.

Ward has compiled that enviable record from only 56 runners and those ten winners give him an 18 per cent strike-rate and a level-stake profit of +48pt.

The bulk of his runners and most of his success

has been in two-year-old races (7-41, 17%, +22.5pt) but he landed Group 1 honours with Undrafted in the 2015 Diamond Jubilee Stakes and two years ago did the same when Lady Aurelia scored a brilliant win in the King's Stand Stakes, following up the previous year's Queen Mary Stakes victory *(below)*.

His growing reputation has seen most of his more recent winners go off at shorter odds. He has had eight outright favourites with results of 01101270 (38%, +3pt) and overall seven of his ten winners have gone off 13-2 or shorter.

Money talks

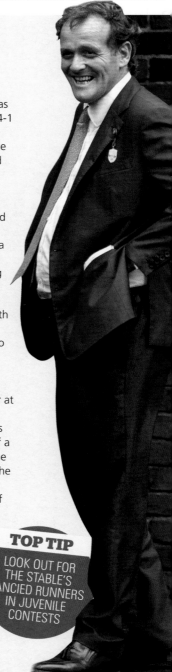

RICHARD HANNON could not have had a better set-up for his training career, having taken the reins at the powerful family stable built up by his father Richard snr, and he grasped the opportunity immediately, not least when he opened his Royal Ascot account in his very first race in 2014 with Toronado's triumph in the Group 1 Queen Anne.

He added another winner that week when Baitha Alga landed the Norfolk Stakes and ended his first season as British champion trainer, succeeding his father as title-holder.

Having completed five years as a trainer, Hannon ranks seventh on the Royal Ascot scoreboard in that time with five winners, although he had a blank last year when the closest he came was Euginio's one-length second to Monarchs Glen in the Wolferton Stakes.

Hannon has followed his father's example of producing early two-year-olds and that is one area worth exploring. Two of his five Royal Ascot winners have been in that age bracket and both were fancied – Baitha Alga was 8-1 and Illuminate was 4-1 favourite in the 2015 Albany Stakes. The stable has a lot of two-year-old runners but the dozen who started under 10-1 have yielded two wins, three seconds and a third (17%, +2pt).

Hannon has had only a handful of favourites at this competitive meeting but the market has proved a good indicator of stable confidence, with his four Group-race favourites producing two wins and a third.

He has had two handicap favourites and one of them, Windshear at 4-1 in the 2014 King George V Handicap, was beaten three-quarters of a length into second by the other joint-favourite in the race.

Last year all but one of his runners was priced at 16-1 or higher, which was a clear signal that his squad was below strength.

It is also worth noting that Hannon has yet to win a race beyond a mile at the meeting.

TOP TIP

LOOK OUT FOR THE STABLE'S FANCIED RUNNERS IN JUVENILE CONTESTS

WINNING IS BLOODLINE, TRAINING, TACTICS, OPTIMUM NUTRITION, EQUINE MINDSET AND SOME LUCK

seracingphoto.co.uk CC Attr2.0 UK

WE OPTIMISE OPTIMUM NUTRITION
01858 464550

ALOERIDE
.com
Best British Aloe Vera by far

Profitable link with Gosden

TOP TIP

KEEP A CLOSE EYE ON FANCIED RUNNERS FOR JOHN GOSDEN AND WESLEY WARD

FRANKIE DETTORI has teamed up to great effect with John Gosden in recent years, landing the Derby and three Prix de l'Arc de Triomphes, and they had a memorable Royal Ascot in 2018 when they combined for four winners.

That marked a triumphant return to Royal Ascot for Dettori, who had been forced to miss the 2017 meeting with an arm injury. Two of his 2018 wins were in Group 1 races with Stradivarius (Gold Cup) and Without Parole (St James's Palace Stakes), while the others came in the Khalid Abdullah colours on Calyx in the Coventry Stakes and Monarchs Glen in the Wolferton Stakes.

Dettori's score now stands at 60 wins, with only six blank years in the near three decades since he rode his first Royal Ascot winner in 1990 at the age of 19. While he has not won the meeting's top jockey award since 2004, having been beaten by Ryan Moore again last year, he is still the meeting's most successful current rider.

Gosden gave him the bulk of his rides last year (15 out of 23) and that is likely to be the case again. They got off to a flying start in 2018 when Calyx, Without Parole and Monarchs Glen – Dettori's only rides on the opening day – all won, and they stayed in the hunt all week with a second, two thirds and two fourths as well as Stradivarius's thrilling Gold Cup triumph.

The other mainstay for Dettori is US trainer Wesley Ward, for whom he has won a Diamond Jubilee on Undrafted and a Queen Mary on the brilliant Lady Aurelia. Ward often brings a rider from the States but is sure to use Dettori when he can, sharing with Gosden an implicit trust in the rider's ability.

At Dettori's last four meetings, he has had 16 rides at 6-1 or less for that pair and they have included five winners and two seconds.

The meeting features 16 races on the straight course and 14 on the round course, and Dettori's even split of 30 wins on

Celebrations last year after Dettori made it 60 winners at Royal Ascot

MOST SUCCESSFUL RACES

Gold Cup
■■■■■■
Queen Anne Stakes
■■■■■■
Ribblesdale Stakes
■■■■■■
Chesham Stakes
■■■■
King Edward VII Stakes
■■■■
Prince of Wales's Stakes
■■■
Sandringham Handicap
■■■
St James's Palace Stakes
■■■

each track is testament to his all-round ability.

Similarly, while there has been plenty of success in sprints, Dettori's six Gold Cups confirm he is just as good over extreme distances. Only ten wins have been in handicaps, but that's not a bad strike-rate considering they are invariably much more open than Group races.

In short, there is no race at a big meeting like Royal Ascot when an owner, trainer or punter would not be happy to have Dettori on board their horse.

23	**7**	**26**	**60**	
ASCOTS AT WHICH DETTORI HAS WON RACES	WINNERS IN 1998 – HIS BEST YEAR	DIFFERENT RACES WON	ROYAL ASCOT WINNERS	*1990* YEAR OF FIRST ROYAL ASCOT WINNER

Master jockey so good at being in right place

R YAN MOORE has been leading rider at Royal Ascot in eight of the past nine years and sets the bar extremely high for anyone who wants to leap above him. Quite simply, there is no better rider on the big occasion anywhere in the world.

Moore has been trusted first by Sir Michael Stoute and latterly by Aidan O'Brien, and it is no coincidence that the top two active trainers at Royal Ascot have made him their main man. Tremendous talent in the saddle will always attract the best horsepower.

By almost any measure Moore outstrips his rivals. In the past five years he has ridden 32 Royal Ascot winners – more than double the 14 of William Buick, his closest rival over that period – and it should not be long before he overtakes Frankie Dettori as the leading active rider at the meeting. With 53 winners, Moore is just seven behind.

Moore's win tally in the past five years is matched

Moore after landing last year's Queen's Vase with Kew Gardens

MOST SUCCESSFUL RACES

Hardwicke Stakes
■■■■■
Queen's Vase
■■■■
Ascot Handicap
■■■
Chesham Stakes
■■■
Duke of Edinburgh Handicap
■■■
Queen Alexandra Stakes
■■■
Ribblesdale Stakes
■■■

2008
YEAR OF FIRST ROYAL ASCOT WINNER

exactly by his number of seconds and thirds, which is a sign not that he falls short too often but that he regularly puts his mounts in a position to win. That means a whopping 44 per cent of Moore's rides at Royal Ascot since 2014 have finished in the top three and 22 per cent were winners.

Seventeen of Moore's 32 winners in the past five years have been favourites, with only three returned at double-figure odds. His biggest-priced winner at Royal Ascot came in the 2017 Norfolk Stakes aboard 14-1 shot Sioux Nation. He is ultra-

MOORE'S ROYAL ASCOT WINNERS BY TRAINER

- ■ Aidan O'Brien **22**
- ■ Sir Michael Stoute 17
- ■ Willie Mullins 5
- ■ William Haggas 2
- ■ Others 7*
- *One each for Clive Brittain, Henry Candy, John Gosden, Mark Johnston, Gary Moore, David Wachman, Wesley Ward

reliable but not necessarily profitable from a betting perspective.

Moore tends to end up on more favourites nowadays, possibly because they are overbet due to his reputation, and his record in the past three years is not good (9-34, 26%, -12.63pt).

A better tactic for punters would be to support him in lower-level races. Since 2012 he has had 33 'outside' rides (other than for O'Brien or Stoute) in non-Group races and seven have won for a healthy strike-rate and profit (21%, +10.5pt).

However, those figures can be boiled down to his link with top jumps trainer Willie Mullins in long-distance races (5-10, 50%, +17.5pt) and bookings for Mullins should always be noted.

Other trainers who have called on Moore's services infrequently but often successfully in the past decade are William Haggas (2-9, +5pt) and Mark Johnston (1-3, +6pt).

53
ROYAL ASCOT WINNERS

26
DIFFERENT RACES WON

9
WINNERS IN 2015, A POST-WAR RECORD

TAKE NOTE WHEN HE RIDES FOR WILLIE MULLINS

TOP TIPS

RECENT LOSSES ON FAVOURITES

Skilful rider of fancies

WILLIAM BUICK has cemented his place as one of the elite big-race riders in his four years on a Godolphin retainer, scoring 11 Royal Ascot wins in that time to move up to fourth on the list of active riders at the meeting.

With a total of 23 winners, Buick is behind only Frankie Dettori, Ryan Moore and Jamie Spencer and, at 30, is the youngest of the quartet, so he looks sure to be a major player at Royal Ascot for years to come.

He has been on the scoreboard at the royal meeting for eight straight years and his record at the past five meetings (14 wins from 122 rides) is bettered only by Moore. His rate of success has quickened under Godolphin, with all but one of his 11 winners since 2015 coming under their banner.

Six of the 11 have been for Charlie Appleby, with whom he also teamed up for Derby glory with Masar last year, and two of those came at the 2018 meeting with Blue Point in the

King's Stand Stakes and Old Persian in the King Edward VII Stakes. At the past four meetings Buick is 4-52 (12%, +15pt) for Appleby, although the profit stems mainly from winners at 16-1 and 20-1.

The other Godolphin scorers were supplied by Richard Fahey (two) and Mark Johnston (two), while Buick's only 'outside' winner came from Marco Botti with Aljazzi in last year's Duke of Cambridge Stakes.

It is worth noting any

STRONG LINKS WITH CHARLIE APPLEBY AND MARK JOHNSTON

TOP TIPS

FANCIED RIDES GO WELL

call-ups by Johnston, who has provided two winners and a third from 11 rides at the past four meetings (+3pt). Those three rides were the shortest-priced Johnston hopes of the 11, so the market is a good guide with this link-up.

In fact, it is a sign of Buick's race craft that last year he was in the shake-up on virtually all his fancied mounts. He was in the first four on eight of the nine below 10-1 and won on two of them for a small level-stake profit.

Jamie Spencer

Winning art of perfect timing

ONLY Frankie Dettori and Ryan Moore among the current crop of riders have partnered more Royal Ascot winners than Spencer, who hit the target twice last year to take his total to 26.

His first win of the 2018 meeting came in trademark style on Agrotera in the Sandringham Handicap as he timed his challenge to perfection on the straight mile to pick off his rivals one by one. Spencer's approach might not be to everyone's taste but it is certainly thrilling when it comes off and it is difficult to argue against its effectiveness given his impressive stats on the straight course in races with huge fields.

Since 2013, in mile or shorter races at all of Ascot's fixtures, Spencer's rides in fields of 16-plus runners have shown a huge profit of +67.50pt (13-92, 14%).

Agrotera's success made it five handicap wins down the straight for Spencer since 2013 (two Sandringhams, two Britannias and a Wokingham) and he went close to another in last year's Wokingham when beaten less than a length

into third on 22-1 shot Major Jumbo, faring best of the high-drawn runners.

Spencer is not affiliated with a particular stable and has won for a wide range of trainers. Nowadays he is worth noting when teaming up with David Simcock (two wins, a second and a third from 13 rides

since 2014), Kevin Ryan (also 13 rides in the same period, for three seconds and four thirds, most at double-figure odds), Jamie Osborne and Ed Walker (Agrotera last year).

There is more to Spencer than straight-course mastery, as he showed with his other win last year on Pallasator *(left)* in the Queen Alexandra Stakes. That was his second success in Royal Ascot's longest race and he has also won the Gold Cup, plus the King Edward VII Stakes twice.

One of the plus points with Spencer is that he often improves the chances of big-priced runners, but he is also reliable on his most fancied rides. At the past five meetings he has had 21 mounts priced at 8-1 or lower and has made the first three on 11 of them, with four winning (19%, +3.5pt).

TOP TIP

TAKE NOTE WHEN HE RIDES IN FIELDS WITH 16 OR MORE RUNNERS ON THE STRAIGHT TRACK

Top-level star

J AMES DOYLE has been on the scoreboard at every Royal Ascot since his breakthrough treble in 2013, memorably headed by Al Kazeem's victory in the Prince of Wales's Stakes, and his total now stands at ten winners.

Last year's two wins included another Prince of Wales's on Poet's Word (*above*), followed later in the week by Main Edition's Albany Stakes victory. Five of his ten wins have come in Group 1 races, leaving no doubt that he is a rider for the big occasion.

Like many up-and-coming riders, Doyle's early chances in the big races were mainly on second-strings and outsiders but the quality of his rides is improving fast and his record on Group 1 mounts at Royal Ascot priced at under 10-1 now stands at 11522011010 (46%, +11.48pt).

In fact, he is generally reliable on any fancied horse. Since 2013 he has had 40 rides under 10-1 and seven have won, with a further 15 in second or third. That's a 12 per cent winning strike-rate and a 55 per cent strike-rate in the first three. Both of last year's winners were in that category, with Poet's Word at 11-2 and Main Edition at 7-1.

Another mark of his growing reputation is that his ten winners have come for ten different trainers, with Sir Michael Stoute and Mark Johnston added to the list last year.

TOP TIP

EXCELLENT ON FANCIED RIDES IN GROUP 1 RACES

Murphy rising fast

ADAM KIRBY

Adam Kirby ranks sixth on the Royal Ascot jockeys' list over the past five years, even though he has had far fewer rides than all the jockeys above him and many of those just below him.

His prowess on the all-weather has taught him to make the most of every mount and, remarkably, he is not far off a break-even figure for all rides at the meeting since 2014. He has had five winners in that period from 69 rides, plus nine others in the first three, even though more than 80 per cent of his mounts have been sent off at double-figure odds.

Having notched his first winner in 2012, his overall total stands at seven and five have been for main supporter Clive Cox. Four of the Cox winners (plus another one) came on the straight course and a speedy sort from that stable is likely to be Kirby's best chance.

ANDREA ATZENI

Andrea Atzeni doubled his Royal Ascot tally to four winners with last year's handicap successes on Lagostovegas in the Ascot Handicap and Baghdad in the King George V Handicap.

That brace added to his wins on Cursory Glance in the 2014 Albany Stakes and Stradivarius in the 2017 Queen's Vase, meaning his four victories have come for different trainers – Roger Varian, John Gosden, Willie Mullins and Mark Johnston.

Last year Atzeni had only six rides priced at 10-1 or lower and won on two of them. With the backing of Varian's ever-improving Newmarket stable and additional support from a range of top trainers, he is likely to find better chances coming his way.

OISIN MURPHY

Oisin Murphy has had just two Royal Ascot winners but that figure looks sure to rise quickly after his breakthrough season at the top level in 2018.

Roaring Lion led the way as Murphy collected nine Group 1 wins in a sparkling season and, at 23, he is the bright new star in the Flat jockey ranks.

He landed his first Royal Ascot victory in 2017 on Benbatl in the Hampton Court Stakes and followed up last year with Signora Cabello in the Queen Mary Stakes. More success cannot be far away, and quite likely his Group 1 breakthrough at the meeting.

SIX TO WATCH

Trainers and jockeys looking for a Royal Ascot breakthrough

OWEN BURROWS

Having worked for Sir Michael Stoute for more than a decade, Burrows, 44, knows exactly what is involved in preparing horses for racing's most fashionable week. Now in his fourth season with a licence, as essentially a private trainer for Hamdan Al Maktoum, the Lambourn handler has bettered his tally of winners each term and assembled a promising string including Laraaib and Wadilsafa.

SEAN DAVIS

Davis, 20, from County Kildare, is seen as a leading contender for the British apprentice title, having impressed since linking up with Richard Fahey towards the end of last year. He burst on to the scene when winning a premier handicap on Maudlin Magdalen at the Curragh in 2016 and made more headlines last summer when scoring at the Galway festival on Safe Voyage. Davis has yet to ride at Royal Ascot but his claim may make him popular with trainers

looking for an edge in the big handicaps.

MICHAEL DODS

Dods, 56, is known for producing high-quality sprint fillies at his Darlington base and has come close to Royal Ascot success, with Easton Angel repelled by US raider Acapulco in the 2015 Queen Mary and Mabs Cross finishing a close third in last year's King's Stand. Having become a Group 1 winner in the Prix de l'Abbaye last autumn, Mabs Cross returns for a second go at being the one to break Dods's duck.

PJ McDONALD

Graham Lee and Jim Crowley are former jump jockeys with Royal Ascot victories on their CVs and it may not be long before McDonald, 36, joins the club. Successful on Hot Weld in the 2007 Scottish Grand National, he switched codes not long after and has surpassed 100 winners in the last two campaigns. His association with Group 1 contenders

Laurens and Invincible Army offers hope of a week to remember.

JOSEPH O'BRIEN

As a jockey O'Brien, 26, won the Queen Anne, Prince of Wales's and Gold Cup and, given the remarkable trajectory of his second career, he is likely to get on the Royal Ascot honours board as a trainer soon. He has won the Irish Derby and Melbourne Cup, as well as striking at this year's Cheltenham Festival, and will have chances from his mix of middle-distance horses, two-year-olds and handicappers.

JASON WATSON

Watson, 19, from Brighton, has come a long way in a short time and was crowned champion apprentice last year. He is now based with Roger Charlton, whose first Royal Ascot winner came in 1992 and has a fine touch when it comes to readying challengers. Impressive London Gold Cup winner Headman is one of their best prospects.